THOR

THOR

ANATOMY OF A WEAPON SYSTEM

GEOFF GOODCHILD

 FONTHILL

Fonthill Media Language Policy

Fonthill Media publishes in the international English language market. One language edition is published worldwide. As there are minor differences in spelling and presentation, especially with regard to American English and British English, a policy is necessary to define which form of English to use. The Fonthill Policy is to use the form of English native to the author. Geoff Goodchild was born and educated in Lincolnshire; therefore British English has been adopted in this publication.

Fonthill Media Limited
Fonthill Media LLC
www.fonthillmedia.com
office@fonthillmedia.com

First published in the United Kingdom and the United States of America 2016
Reprinted 2021

British Library Cataloguing in Publication Data:
A catalogue record for this book is available from the British Library

Typeset in 10.5pt on 13pt Minion Pro
Printed and bound in England

Acknowledgements

During my research, I have been afforded the great privilege of meeting and communicating with a wide range of 'Thor's people'—from those who were 'in on the ground floor' at the secret meetings in the old school house in Inglewood, California (where Thor was conceived), to those who operated and maintained the system with the RAF and USAF. I have found it a deeply humbling experience and have developed a very great respect for all those people who were 'Thor'.

I have received invaluable help from many people who have given freely of their time and resources in assisting me to trace the technical aspects of Thor. Clearly, someone has to be first in the list and someone has to be last; however, all have made a significant contribution to my research. Some have become friends and some are, sadly, no longer with us. To them all, I am deeply grateful.

I am particularly indebted to the late Col. Edward N. Hall, USAF, Thor Project Director, for his help and advice and making introductions on my behalf; the late Col. (Dr) B. P. (Paul) Blasingame, USAF, Head of the Guidance and Control Group, Inglewood, for a rare insight into the days at Inglewood, the competing techniques for Thor's guidance system, and making introductions; and the late Mr Paul O. Larson, AC Spark Plug, Chief Engineer, Thor guidance system. Paul was at Inglewood and later in England with Project Emily and went on to work in many projects, including Apollo. He was awarded the Presidential Medal of Freedom for his contribution to the safe return of the Apollo 13 astronauts. Paul gave much of his time, resources, and enthusiasm in helping me to gain something of an understanding of the art of navigating a missile. My appreciation also goes to Lt-Col. Tom Hafner, USAF (Retired) AO 106 (SM) Sqn, later ICBM Force, for his time and very great help with missile systems, launch control, and Thor in general; Sqn Ldr Frank Leatherdale, DFC, RAF (Retired), OC 220 (SM) Sqn, for his great help and advice on all things Thor; Chief Technician W. 'Bill' Roseby, RAF (Retired), 113 (SM) Sqn, for his encyclopaedic knowledge and tireless help with the practical aspects of Thor operations; Sqn Ldr Bill Young, RAF (Retired), OC 82 (SM) Sqn, who provided a very detailed insight into the operational aspects of launching a Thor and very generously presented me with his personal collection of Thor photography; Mr John Birkett of Lincoln for a mine of Thor information and memorabilia; Maj. Rob Leese, USAF, SAF/PAO at the Pentagon, for his very great help with permissions to draw from official sources; and to my eldest son, Tim, who made the chance remark that led to this book being written, for his contribution with his image wizardry, and for being a tireless sounding board, advisor, and researcher.

I am also very grateful for the contributions of Malcolm Leslie, MT Driver (Heavy); Dennis Thomas, Thor Electrical, 98 (SM) Sqn, for his help with things electrical; and Flt Lt Bill Meichan, RAF (Retd), and Flt Lt Roy Matthews, RAF (Retd), both LCOs from 220 (SM) Sqn, consulted on my behalf by Sqn Ldr Leatherdale.

My most grateful thanks go to Col. Charlie Simpson, USAF (Retired), Executive Director, Association of Air Force Missileers and Scott Matson USAF, (Retired), ICBM Force, for effecting introductions; Bill Hunt, Ministry of Defence negative librarian for tirelessly searching the archives; Peter Elliott, RAF Museum, London, for imagery and site plans; Wayne Cocroft of English Heritage for imagery and general Thor information; Mr Morris Poucher, for kindly allowing me access to his Thor site at Bardney in order to make detailed drawings and diagrams; Mr Brian Rice, for access to the Harrington site; Mr David Wilmot-Smith for access to and guiding me around the Breighton Thor and Stage One sites; and to Carol and Jim at the RAF Museum, Cosford, for their help on my recent visit to the Thor exhibit.

Special thanks must go to Joshua Greenland of Fonthill Media for his careful editing and help in seeing this book into print.

Finally, any number of thanks is nowhere near enough of a reward for my long suffering partner Jan and our two sons, Jacob and Sheridan, who have lived most of their lives in not so much of a house as a Thor squadron crew room.

Geoff Goodchild
Northamptonshire, March 2016

Glossary of Terms

AC	Alternating current.
Accelerometer	A mechanical device to measure the acceleration of a body or object.
Actuator	A mechanical device, which moves proportionally to the hydraulic effort placed upon it.
Altitude	The vertical distance above the earth (usually measured in feet for aeronautical purposes).
Amplidyne	An amplifier system that allows small electrical signals to drive very large motors with high precision. See amplifier.
Amplifier	A circuit that increases a signal's voltage into a higher one so tiny changes can be detected more easily.
Angle of Attack or AoA	The angle between the reference line of a missile and the airflow relative to it.
Arcminute/Arcsecond	Scientific measurements for extremely small angles: 1 arcminute = 1/60th of a degree; 1 arcsecond = 1/3,600th of a degree.
ARL	Army Research Laboratory.
Attitude	The position of a missile as determined by the inclination of its axes (roll, pitch, and yaw) in relation to another object, such as the earth.
Autopilot	An automated system of flight control.
AWMD	Air Ministry Works Directorate.
Axis	A line about which an object, device, or system rotates (e.g., X, Y, or Z).
BOC	British Oxygen Company.
CEA	Control and electronics assembly—part of the missile's flight control system.
CEP	Circular error probable—military term for the accuracy of a warhead, based on the area in which it will land 50 per cent of the time, with the average being the centre point of the circle.

Cycles	The speed at which an electrical waveform changes over time. See Hertz.
DC	Direct current, for example the electrical force produced by batteries.
Degree or Deg.	Standard unit of measurement of an angle: 1 Degree = 1/360th of a complete circle.
EET	Electrical equipment trailer. Part of the ground support equipment. See GSE.
FCS	Flight control system. System for controlling the missile's flight path (trajectory).
FMCC	Food, Machinery and Chemical Corporation. An American contractor that developed the transporter/erector vehicle. See TEL
fps	feet per second, an aeronautical measurement of speed.
GE	General Electric, the contractor that built the RV.
Gimbal	A point about which a mechanical system or object rotates.
Gimbal Gain	A measurement of a gyroscope's sensitivity.
GN2	Nitrogen gas, used for pressurisation of flight systems and fuel tanks.
GPO	General Post Office (precursor to British Telecom)
GSE	Ground support equipment. A series of trailers that contained important electrical and mechanical systems—used to maintain the missile's on-board components.
Gyro or Gyroscope	A mechanical device with a spinning wheel or rotor. Used to provide stability or a reference direction in flight control and navigation systems.
Hertz or Hz	A measurement of how quickly an alternating current changes per second. See Cycle.
HPT	Hydro-pneumatic trailer—part of Thor's ground equipment. See GSE.
Hydraulic	A system that uses high-pressure liquid to achieve a mechanical effect.
IBM	International Business Machines. An organisation that pioneered early scientific computers.
ICBM	Inter-Continental Ballistic Missile (e.g., Titan and Atlas).
IGS	Inertial guidance system.
Inverter	An electro-mechanical device that converts low-voltage battery DC power into high-voltage AC current. See AC and DC.

IRBM	Intermediate Range Ballistic Missile (e.g. Thor).
kt	Kiloton, a measurement of the explosive power of a nuclear warhead. Equivalent to 1,000 tonnes of TNT. See TNT.
LCA	Launch control area.
LCCO Panel	Launch control console operator's panel.
LCO Panel	Launch control officer's panel.
LCT	Launch control trailer.
LE	Launch emplacement.
LOX or LO2	Common abbreviation for liquid oxygen.
LRT	Long-range electro-theodolite. A complex, electro-optical device that was used to maintain the stabilised platform's alignment.
Max-q	The point at which the aerodynamic stresses on a body as it travels through the atmosphere are greatest.
MCOT	Missile check-out trailer. Wheeled onto the pad when diagnostics and testing of the missile's systems where required. Normally parked on the LCA.
MECO	Main engine cut-off.
MIT	Massachusetts Institute of Technology.
MMIA	Mueller Mechanical Integrating Accelerometer. A device used in the V-2 rocket. Developed for use in later missiles. See V-2, PIGA.
Motor-Generator or M-G	An electro-mechanical device that uses rotational motion to convert a DC electrical source into three-phase AC.
mt	Megaton, a measurement of the explosive power of a nuclear warhead. Equivalent to 1,000,000 tonnes of TNT. See TNT.
NDT	Nitrogen distribution trailer. See GSE.
Null	The zero or centre point about which a system comes to rest when no inputs are placed upon it.
Oblate Spheroid	The approximate shape of the earth. See Q-Guidance.
PAL	Permissive action link. A method for preventing warheads from being detonated without the proper authorisation.
PCMA	Pneumatic control manifold assembly—a system on the launch emplacement that controlled the flow of pressurised gas.
PDT	Power distribution trailer. Contained distribution systems for a pad's electrical power. Located on the LCA adjacent to the LCT.

PIGA	Pendulous integrating gyroscope accelerometer—a device that measures the change of velocity of an object or body about a particular axis with extreme accuracy. See Gyro, Axis.
Pneumatic	A system that uses high-pressure gas to achieve a mechanical effect.
POL Store	Petrol, oil, and lubricants store. Standard military term for an area that contains flammable liquids.
Potentiometer	An electro-mechanical device that outputs a differential voltage relative to a position about an axis.
Programmer	The part of the missile's flight control system that operated for the first stage of flight. See Autopilot.
PSI	Pounds per square inch. Standard units for measuring pressure.
PTS	Propellant transfer system. A series of pipes and valves that controlled the flow of propellants from the storage tanks to the missile during fuelling. See Valve Complex.
Pyro or Pyrotechnics	Small explosive devices that are usually electrically initiated.
Q-Guidance and Q-Matrix	The set of mathematical equations that give rise to the guidance system's ability to target a specific point on the earth's surface.
Radian or Rad	Standard unit of measurement of an angle: 1 Radian = 57.2958 degrees. See Degree.
RAF	Royal Air Force.
Relay	An electrically operated switch that controls high-voltage circuits safely.
Resolver	An electro-mechanical device that measures the angle between two points with high accuracy.
RIM	Receipt, inspection, and maintenance building.
RP-1	The fuel used by Thor's engines.
RP-1 Computer	The electro-mechanical system that determined the amount of fuel loaded into the missile based on environmental considerations such as temperature and air pressure. Formed part of the PTS.
rpm	Revolutions per minute.
RV	Re-entry vehicle. The part of the missile that contains the warhead.
SAC	Strategic Air Command.

Servo	A mechanical device which moves as a result of a control signal being fed to it.
SIBS	Stellar inertial bombing system. A method of using the position of stars to update navigation systems and guide aircraft onto a target with extreme accuracy.
Single Phase or 1-Phase	Alternating current that contains just one waveform.
SM	Strategic missile.
Squib	A pyrotechnic device. See Pyro.
SRT	Short-range electro-theodolite. An electro-optical device that was used to align the missile's guidance system before launch.
Stabilised Platform	The part of the missile's guidance system where the accelerometers were placed. It was stabilised by gyroscopes.
Synchro or Synchronous Motor	A method of transmitting the angle of a motor's shaft to another shaft via electrical wires with a very high level of accuracy.
TEL	Transporter-erector-launcher. The articulated trailer upon which the missile was transported and stored.
Three-Phase	Alternating current that contains three waveforms, spaced 90 degrees apart from each other.
TNT	Tri-Nitro-Toluene, a type of high explosive.
Transducer	A sensor that measures small changes of angles relative to an object and converts them into an electrical signal.
Transformer	An electrical device that changes the voltage of a circuit.
Turbopump	A gas-powered pump that delivers very high rates of flow.
USAF	United States Air Force.
V-2	German ballistic missile used in the Second World War.
Valve	Mechanical devices that allow or impede flow of a liquid or gas.
Valve Complex	A series of valves and control systems that allowed the missile to be fuelled and de-fuelled safely. See PTS.
Vc, Vg, and Vm	Measurements of velocity used by the guidance system. See Q-Guidance.

VECO	Vernier engine cut-off.
Velocity	Speed and direction of an object as it travels through the atmosphere, typically measured in feet per second for ballistic objects. See fps.
VSE	Vertical sensing element. A form of electronic 'spirit level' within the missile.
W-49	The model name for the warhead.

CONTENTS

Introduction

Being born and raised in rural Lincolnshire in the early 1950s, it was impossible to avoid the sights and sounds of all that the Royal Air Force had to offer. Lincolnshire, in common with most of the eastern side of the UK was dotted with virtually intact airfields left over from the mighty bomber offensives of the not too distant Second World War. One such airfield, not far from my home, was soon to become a hive of activity once again, having been selected as one of the four satellite sites for the Hemswell Thor complex. There was little to see, until one ordinary day, for which, despite the daily visual treats of the latest in military hardware, this schoolboy was not even remotely prepared—the sight, from close range, of a retracting shelter followed by the almost magical rising of a gleaming white missile to the vertical. Thor had arrived. That awesome first 'close encounter' lives on in memory with remarkable clarity, and such was its effect that it instantly instilled a deep-rooted interest that has never subsided. A chance comment, made while walking over the remains of that very same launch site over thirty years later, began the long quest to discover and document the technical achievement that was Thor.

The SM (Strategic Missile) 75 Thor was an interim measure, intended to 'plug' a perceived missile gap between Russia and the United States, pending the introduction of the Atlas intercontinental ballistic missile. Produced as a fully integrated weapon system by the Douglas Aircraft Company under contract WS-315A, Thor was based in the UK and jointly manned by American and British personnel. This 'dual key' arrangement, which satisfied political issues on both sides of the Atlantic, called for the custody and control of the nuclear warhead to be retained by the United States Air Force, while the missile system would be 'owned' by the Royal Air Force. Active participation of both nations would therefore be required to render the weapon system viable.

Thor looked set to pave the way for future generations of ballistic missiles operated by the Royal Air Force, but with the cancellation of the Blue Streak medium-range ballistic missile in April 1960 and its successor, the Skybolt, in December 1962, this was destined to be the only period that the RAF would operate such a weapon. Thor left squadron service in the UK in 1963, and for a great deal of the time since then, it has been in danger of slipping into total obscurity. It was the observation of this rather sad reflection on such an important part of the UK's military heritage that prompted the earlier-mentioned comment.

This book focusses on the technical aspects of Thor and is intended to provide a detailed description of the system as based in the UK. The information it contains has been gathered over a very long period. Some is from official sources, as and when it became available, the majority having come from the resources and recollections of some of those who knew the system intimately. Some information, which could not be verified or agreed by consensus, has been omitted. For any omissions, or errors that may remain, please accept my apologies.

Despite focusing on the technical aspects, my research soon revealed that any history of Thor is as much about her people as the weapon system itself. The short period between the initial concept of Thor and her deployment in eastern England under the code name of Project Emily was an exceptionally turbulent ride for those involved. There were those who conceived the idea, those who worked endlessly to produce and install the system and those who maintained their, often, lonely vigil on the operational Thor sites scattered in the English countryside. This, the first deployment of an operational ballistic missile system in the western world, was indeed a unique period, and to this unique band of people, some of whom gave their lives in the service of Thor, this work is dedicated.

1

The Sites

The Site

The Thor strategic missile force was divided into four separate wings, each with a main base and four satellite sites. This arrangement of the individual wings was referred to as a complex. The main bases were established on current RAF stations because, with the already existing infrastructure (such as hangars and accommodation for personnel), the time and cost of conversion to their new role would be at a minimum. The stations chosen as main bases were RAF Feltwell, Norfolk; RAF Hemswell, Lincolnshire; RAF Driffield, Yorkshire; and RAF North Luffenham, Rutland. The Driffield and Hemswell complexes came under the control of No. 1 Group, Bomber Command, while the remaining complexes were under No. 3 Group.

Each complex was armed with fifteen missiles, with three hosted at a launch site within the main base, the remaining twelve being divided equally between the four remote satellite sites. The selection criteria for the remote sites included the existence of suitable roads between the main base and the sites and their distance from the main base and each other. This method of dispersal ensured that a separate attack would be required on each of the sites in order to render the Thor force wholly ineffective.

The satellite launch sites were constructed on airfields left over from the Second World War, of which there were still many, and which remained in government ownership. There were several alternative plans considered for the basing of Thor, the final selection appearing in the table below.

Main Base	Satellite Sites			
Feltwell	Shepherds Grove	Tuddenham	Mepal	North Pickenham
Hemswell	Bardney	Caistor	Coleby Grange	Ludford Magna
Driffield	Catfoss	Carnaby	Breighton	Full Sutton
North Luffenham	Harrington	Polebrook	Melton Mowbray	Folkingham

Three of the sites, Feltwell, Caistor, and Coleby Grange, were built on all-grass airfields. Carnaby, originally designed as an emergency landing ground for returning bombers making landfall in the North of England, possessed a massive single runway; it was, possibly, the most interestingly configured of all the sites, placed within a circular taxiway and dispersal area to the south of the runway at the south-western end of the airfield. The remaining sites were all built on the standard three-runway bomber type of airfield, and the launch emplacements on these were positioned so as to facilitate the use of existing taxiways, runways, and dispersals as access roads for the transporter/erector, other vehicular equipment and trailers. This feature alone accounted for the non-uniformity of Thor site layout. In order to provide a good road surface around the site and as Thor was an interim measure, it was sufficient to simply lay a suitably wide layer of new tarmac on top of the old concrete. The emplacements themselves required some slight modification to accommodate the points of access at which the existing and new surfaces met; notwithstanding this, however, careful observation will reveal slight differences in the design of the launch emplacements between some complexes. Although RAF North Luffenham was of a three-runway layout, the launch site was constructed just away from the airfield itself in an open area to the south of the main runway, at the eastern end of the airfield.

The contrast in site design of the all-grass and standard three-runway airfields is clearly illustrated by the aerial photographs, both taken from a Vickers Valiant of 543 Squadron at 30,000 feet on 5 May 1964.

Coleby Grange, home to 142 (SM) Squadron with launch emplacements 25, 26, and 27, was a former grass airfield, consequently requiring all site facilities to be built anew. Arguably, this may have made life a little easier for those planning the sites. The security fencing arrangement can be clearly seen, along with the perimeter lighting posts just inside the inner fence. The more prominent white squares are the bases of the theodolite target pillars. The classified storage building and the pyro store, in their revetment at the bottom of the picture, show clearly as do the above-ground cable ducts to the emplacements. The arrangement of the site buildings is also readily apparent and it is possible to identify each of the buildings by referring to the descriptions in this chapter. The faint lines under the surface around the emplacements are the fire-fighting ring main.

The last Thor site, that at Folkingham, with pads 58, 59, and 60 belonging to 223 (SM) Squadron, did benefit from the possession of existing hard surfaces on which to build. The modification of the centre pad is typical of those seen at other sites. As in the Coleby Grange photograph, all elements of the site are clearly identifiable, the fire ring main and one of the static water tanks being particularly prominent. A static water tank and its associated pump housing also feature as the structure nearest to the camera on the general site photograph showing the new road surface laid over the existing taxiway.

Before construction of the launch sites could begin, each of the chosen sites were subjected to detailed astro-geodetic surveys from both within the launch site area and from outside. Geodetics, a branch of applied mathematics and earth sciences, is a scientific discipline that deals with the measurement and representation of the earth, including its gravitational field, in a three-dimensional time-varying space.

The much-assumed perfectly spherical Earth is a Pythagorean concept. It is easy to work with mathematically and, for most practical purposes, is actually accurate enough. For the targeting and launch of ballistic missiles, however, there is a need to be rather more precise and certain other factors have to be accounted for. Earth, rather than being a perfect sphere, is in fact an oblate spheroid, being more of a tangerine shape, flattened a little at the poles, and bulging slightly in the middle regions. This flattening process is caused by the rotation of the Earth and the flattening ratio, as a matter of passing interest only, is 1:298.25. Additionally, the true vertical at a location does not correspond with the theoretical vertical because of the topography and the fact that all geological masses disturb the Earth's gravitational field.

During the survey, in addition to fixing the position of the launch emplacements, other specific points on the launch sites were sighted in by celestial observation. These points were the location of the theodolite target pillars, which provided a permanent reference in relation to true north and were used in the setting up and checking of the guidance system. They will be discussed under guidance in the Launch Emplacement section.

The British Director of Military Surveys was responsible for the survey works outside the sites, while the Americans of the 1381st Geodetic Survey Squadron (Missile) from Orlando Air Force Base, Florida, completed the process inside the Feltwell and Hemswell complexes. The work at the Driffield and North Luffenham complexes was handed over to the Air Ministry Works Directorate.

The ground was broken to begin works for the first complex at Feltwell on 12 May 1958, with that at the Hemswell, Driffield, and North Luffenham beginning on 17 July 1958, 22 December 1958, and 16 April 1959 respectively. During the works, the four complexes required the excavation of some 600,000 cubic yards (458,733 cubic metres) of material and the provision of 400,000 cubic yards (305,822 cubic metres) of selected fill, 80,000 cubic yards (61,164 cubic metres) of base concrete, 60,000 cubic yards (45,873 cubic metres) of vibrated concrete, and 90,000 cubic yards (68,810 cubic metres) of high quality concrete, along with 36,000 feet (10,973 metres) of steel rails. Some sites, due to their geology, required piling in order to provide deep foundations that would ensure stability and the maintenance of the exacting level tolerances to which the launch emplacements were constructed. To this end, some 490 piles were used. The Feltwell complex was completed by December 1958, followed by Hemswell on 30 April 1959, Driffield on 29 September 1959, and North Luffenham on 28 January 1960.

The works carried out at each launch site included the provision of water and electrical power by the utility providers and communications, which, apart from radio links, were provided by GPO telephones. The major structures of the sites were the launch emplacements, launch control area, classified storage building, pyro store, mechanical and electrical plant building, fire tender garages, and the site roads. Strict parameters in the relative positions of certain structures needed to be observed, mostly for safety reasons. In their usually fairly remote rural locations, the sites were not normally that close to any human habitation, but there was a requirement that no missile should be within 1,500 feet (457 metres) of an inhabited dwelling or 750 feet (229 metres) of a public road. Missiles were sited to be at least 700 feet (213 metres) from each other, while the launch control trailer, squadron headquarters and guardroom, and the classified storage building locations were located to achieve the same distance from any missile. Some other siting criteria were more to solve practical issues. For example, the crew room in the headquarters hut should be within 200 feet (61 metres) of the launch control area, turning circles on site should have a minimum radius of 50 feet (15 metres), and a very important issue that the length of cabling required between the missiles and the launch control trailer should not exceed 1,500 feet (457 metres). This is because the Thor equipment came from Douglas as identical kits, and while it is easy to shorten the length of a cable run, it was not possible to increase it. This accounts for some odd-looking shapes appearing in the above-ground concrete-cable ducting. The cables were thick and could not be simply folded to cause an apparent shortening of their length. The solution was to increase the overall length of the ducting by inserting dumbbell-shaped ducts around which the cable could be laid.

The site perimeter was secured by a chain-link, or diamond-mesh, fence that was woven from vertical steel wires, bent into a zigzag pattern. Each wire link, woven with similar neighbouring wires, formed a continuous width of fence possessing the diamond-shaped pattern after which it is named. Concrete posts, spaced at approximately 8-foot (2.5-metre) intervals, provided support for the fence. The posts were vertical to approximately 7 feet 8 inches (2.33 metres) above the ground, after which the top angled out at 45 degrees away from the site for a distance of 2 feet (61 cm) and carried three single strands of barbed wire. The outward angle of the fence posts served to not only increase the overall height, but also created an overhang that would present some difficulties to anyone attempting to climb it. The advantages of the chain-link fence were that it was relatively low cost, but perhaps more importantly, with a mind to its application, this type of fence is transparent and therefore does not cast significant shadows; consequently, potential intruders would be both relatively easily noticed and denied protection. The original Thor site specification called for the fence to be no closer than 150 feet to any launch emplacement, with 200 feet being preferred. This distance was no doubt to counter the throwing of a device such as a grenade from outside of the site perimeter. Inside the site, approximately 12 feet (3.66 metres) back from the fence were the perimeter lighting posts, approximately 100 feet (30.5 metres) apart. These appear to have been of the Mercury Vapour type, as used for street lighting in many towns at that time. They emitted a light that, while essentially white, possessed a distinctive blue-green tint. These lights, in association with the floodlighting at each launch emplacement and the LCA, gave a Thor site, observed at night, the appearance of a bluish-green oasis in the dark rural countryside; from a high vantage point, such as the Lincolnshire Wolds, the site could be seen for many miles. Vehicular access to the site was through a pair of gates protecting the only opening in the fence. The gates were each 7 feet 10 inches (2.4 metres) square, covered by diamond-mesh and topped with barbed wire.

The perimeter fence was, initially, considered to be un-climbable, but this was soon proven not to be the case. An additional fence was therefore provided, parallel to and designed to be 225 feet (68.6 metres) from the original perimeter fence. This new outer fence, which took the form of three coils of barbed wire, two side-by-side with the third placed on top, was approximately 5 feet (1.52metres) high and provided a sterile area that was brought to a close at the sides of road on the approach to the site gates. RAF police dogs would patrol inside this area at night.

Most of the equipment associated directly with the operation of the missile was trailer mounted and positioned at pre-determined points on the launch emplacement or launch control area. Other buildings on the site, such as the squadron headquarters building, the offsite vehicle shelter and the crew chief and technical storage hut, were all of temporary Type 'B' hutting construction, while the LCA annex was a Terrapin-type building. The remaining buildings and structures were of more permanent construction and this accounts for some of these still surviving, in various states, today. The main bases required the conversion of two hangars, one as a receipt, inspection and maintenance (RIM) building, the other for technical storage. The classified storage building at a main base launch site also differed slightly in that it had a two-bay building as opposed to the single bay provided at the satellite sites.

Despite extensive searches, it has not been possible to acquire copies of plans for the individual buildings; however, the author was extremely fortunate to be granted access to a near intact site at the beginning of his research, enabling the production of a set of detailed drawings, which are reproduced in this chapter.

The Site Buildings

Below is a list of Air Ministry Directorate of Works drawing numbers, taken from the site plans in the author's collection:

Air Ministry Directorate of Works Drawing Numbers

Vehicle Shelter
10979A-58   Type B   Hutting

Crew Room   (SHQ)
4069C-58   Type B   Hutting

Fire Tender Garages
7776A-58   Brick and Block

M and E Plant Room
7789B-58   Brick

Fuel Oil Catchpit
7523A-58   Brick and Block

Water tank (20,000 gallons)
7564A-58   Concrete

Water Tank (10,000 gallons)
EP-980-60   Concrete

Launch Emplacement and LRT Building
2908E-58   Concrete
4526E-58   Blocks

Classified Storage Building
4077A-58   Steel and Hyrib

Pyro Store
4078B-58   Steel and Hyrib

Target Pillar
6195C-58   Concrete Tube

Electricity Intake Sub-Station
4431A-58   Brick

Crew Chief and Tech Storage Hut (30 × 18)
EP-683-59   Type B   Hutting

Crew Chief Building (10 × 18)
EP-681-59   PB

POL Storage Building
11704-59H   Blocks

LCT Annex (22 × 18)

RWE-DRI-27   Terrapin Hut

Electrical Distribution Centre 'A' No Drawing

Married Officers Quarter
3127A-56   Type 4 Det. S. Ent   Brick construction
5545-59E   Garage and store   Brick construction

Squadron Headquarters

The squadron headquarters building was of Type B sectional hutting construction—the former 220 (SM) Squadron at North Pickenham, Norfolk, was the subject photographed by the author. At the time of the author's site visit in June 2002, the building was in relatively good condition, with the original main gates intact and in daily use. By 2006, the building and the gates had been removed. This building measured 111 feet (29.13 metres) long by 18 feet 9 inches (5.7 metres) wide. The rear of the building extended beyond the site fencing, this off-site portion incorporating the guardroom. There was a doorway immediately before the fence to enable personnel to enter the site from outside the perimeter, pass through the guardroom, and into the site through a doorway immediately behind the fence. Access was through a turnstile; this was operated by the RAF Police once the necessary identification formalities were completed.

The front section of the building (some 28 feet 5 inches (8.66 metres) long and 18 feet 9 inches (5.7 m) wide) was a dining hall and a partitioned rest area for the NCOs and other ranks. Immediately behind this, on the right-hand side of the building when facing forward into the site, came the kitchen (13 feet 10 inches (4.22 metres) long by 13 feet 8 inches (4.17 metres) wide. Adjoined to the other end of the kitchen was the officers' dining room, the same width as the kitchen and measuring 8 feet (2.44 metres) long. A serving hatch was provided from the kitchen into both dining areas. Filling the remaining width along this length was a corridor, which, at the end of the officers' dining room, changed direction to eventually run down the centre of the building. This change in direction coincided with the position of two doorways, one on each side of the building—one leading out onto the site road and the other to a building of similar size and construction that was occupied by the Air Ministry Works Directorate. Examination of site plans reveals that remote Thor sites sharing their host airfields with stage-one Bloodhound Surface to Air Missile sites, namely Breighton and Carnaby, did not have this feature, this being provided on the stage-one site, which were of a more permanent nature than those associated with Thor. Presumably, the AMWD staff looked after the requirements for both sites.

Following the corridor and facing the rear of the building, the left-hand side provided the location for the latrines, while the commanding officer's office was on the right. Between this point and the guardroom were administration offices, an interview room, stores, and the telephone and telecommunications equipment. The guardroom, approximately 12 feet (3.7 metres) in length and the 18 feet 9 inches (5.7m) wide, completed the squadron headquarters. The guardroom stayed in contact with the RAF Police personnel out on the site by means of a radio link, manufactured by Pye Radio Limited—the mobile unit was worn as a backpack with a whip aerial, a far cry from the small handheld units of today. The remote sites and their wing headquarters were also in contact by VHF radio.

Fire Tender Garage

The fire tender garage had two bays, one being very slightly narrower than the other and more restricted in height, having a 'lean-to' style roof. This latter bay would most likely be utilised to provide parking for a police Land Rover.

Mechanical and Electrical Plant Building

The mechanical and electrical plant building housed the equipment to convert the British 50-Hz utility power to 60 Hz for the operation of Thor's equipment. The

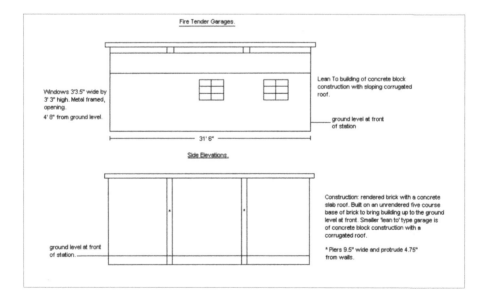

Fire Tender Garages.

Windows 3'3.5" wide by 3' 3" high. Metal framed, opening. 4' 8" from ground level.

Lean To building of concrete block construction with sloping corrugated roof.

ground level at front of station

31' 6"

Side Elevations.

ground level at front of station.

Construction: rendered brick with a concrete slab roof. Built on an unrendered five course base of brick to bring building up to the ground level at front. Smaller 'lean to' type garage is of concrete block construction with a corrugated roof.

* Piers 9.5" wide and protrude 4.75" from walls.

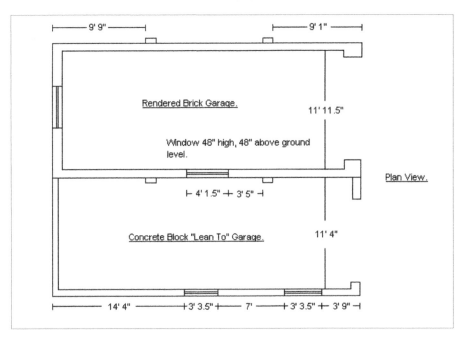

Rendered Brick Garage.

Window 48" high, 48" above ground level.

Plan View.

Concrete Block "Lean To" Garage.

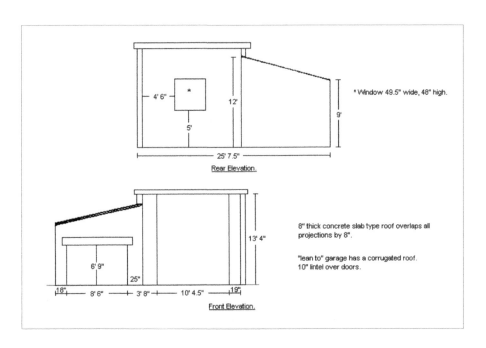

Rear Elevation.

* Window 49.5" wide, 48" high.

8" thick concrete slab type roof overlaps all projections by 8".

"lean to" garage has a corrugated roof. 10" lintel over doors.

Front Elevation.

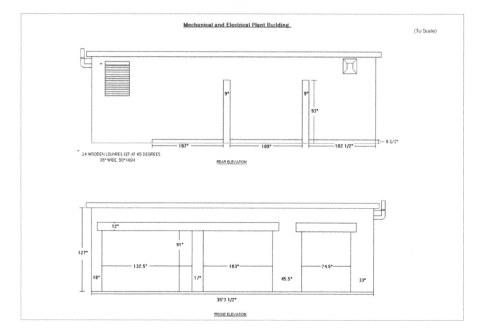

equipment to achieve this was reported to be motor-generators. The UK power would be used to run an electric motor that would, in turn, drive an alternator at a speed that gave an output of the required voltage and frequency. Belt drives or shaft coupling could achieve the connection between the motor and generator. One advantage of this technique was that the input and output sources were electrically isolated. There would be sufficient equipment to provide a redundant capability.

The site standby generator occupied the smaller of the two rooms in the building. Ventilation louvres were provided in the rear wall of the room, while the generator exhaust extension exited the building above and to the rear of the window. The three concrete pads, separated by walls, at the rear of the building were most likely to support transformers for the high voltage of the incoming utility supply to the site.

Static Water Tanks

Fire cover at the launch sites was initially provided by an onsite fire tender. This was, however, soon deemed to be an inadequate arrangement and modifications were made to provide a ring main and hydrant system, providing water that was electrically pumped from two static water tanks to hydrants placed at locations around the site.

The static water tanks provided approximately 30,000 gallons in total and were generally of different capacities, one of 20,000 gallons (90,800 litres) and a smaller

Mechanical and Electrical Plant Room.

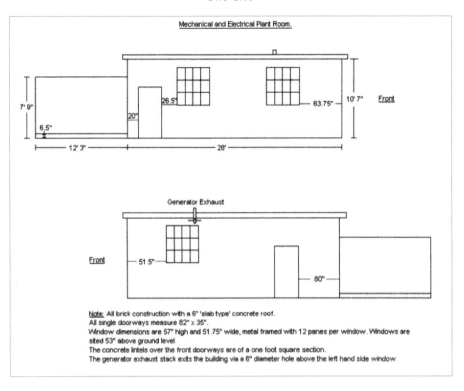

Note: All brick construction with a 6" 'slab type' concrete roof.
All single doorways measure 82" x 35".
Window dimensions are 57" high and 51.75" wide, metal framed with 12 panes per window. Windows are sited 53" above ground level.
The concrete lintels over the front doorways are of a one foot square section.
The generator exhaust stack exits the building via a 6" diameter hole above the left hand side window

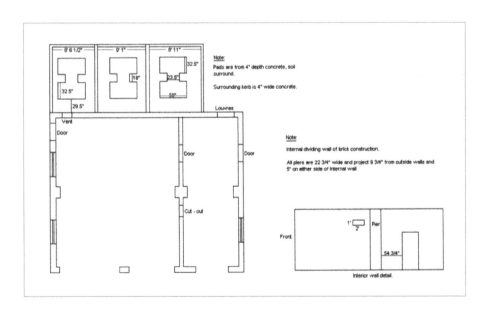

tank of 10,000 gallons (45,400 litres). Although the overall total of water available remained the same, there were differences at some sites; at Carnaby, for example, the site plan shows two identical 15,000 gallons (68,100 litres) tanks.

The 20,000-gallon capacity tank examined by the author measured 30 feet (9.14 metres) square with a depth of 3 feet 6 inches (1.07 metres), 1 foot (30.5 cm) of which was above the nominal ground level. The concrete walls of the tank were 8 inches (20.3 cm) thick. Approximately 4 feet (1.22 metres) from the tank was a small brick-built structure, 4 feet by 7 feet and 3 feet 6 inches high (1.22 m X 2.13 m X 1.07 m), which would house the associated pump.

Classified Storage Building

The classified storage building was used to store any warheads that had been removed from the missiles. It was situated in an 'E' or 'F'-shaped revetment, which it shared with the pyro store.

Pyro Store

The pyro (pyrotechnic) store was for storage of items such as igniter squibs for the engines, latch squibs, and retro rockets.

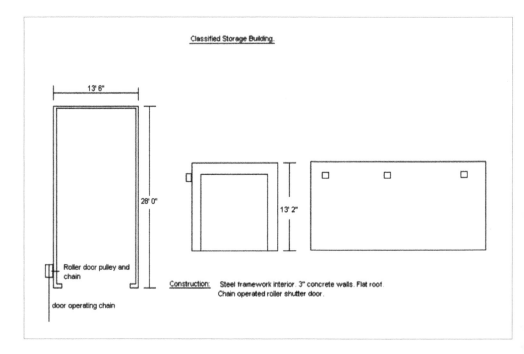

Classified Storage Building.

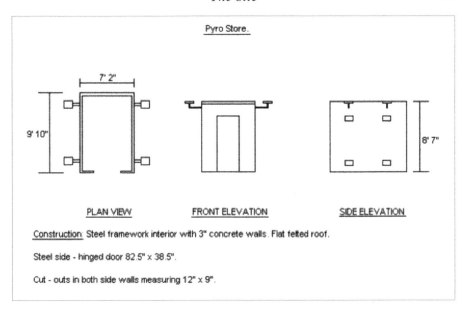

Pyro Store.

PLAN VIEW   FRONT ELEVATION   SIDE ELEVATION

Construction: Steel framework interior with 3" concrete walls. Flat felted roof.

Steel side - hinged door 82.5" x 38.5".

Cut - outs in both side walls measuring 12" x 9".

Petrol, Oil and Lubricants (POL) Store

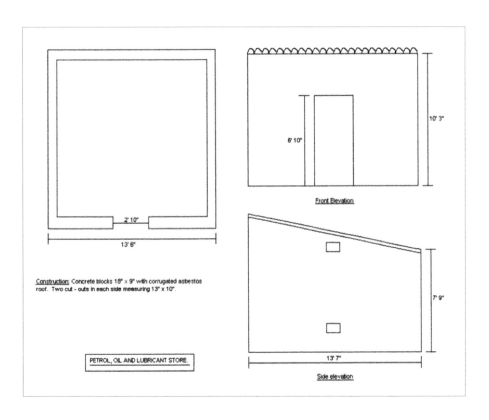

Construction: Concrete blocks 18" x 9" with corrugated asbestos roof. Two cut - outs in each side measuring 13" x 10".

PETROL, OIL AND LUBRICANT STORE.

Front Elevation

Side elevation

Married Officers' Quarter

The accommodation for Thor squadron personnel was generally at the main wing headquarters; consequently, for those based at the outlying satellite squadrons, this involved an often, quite long commute by station transport before and after their planned shift. As a result of this, some personnel elected to live closer to the site and make their own travel arrangements. In respect of the squadron commanding officer, however, a decision had been made that it would be desirable for this officer to reside in close proximity to his command and therefore be within easy reach of the squadron at all times. To that end, land was acquired locally to each remote site for the construction of a married officers' quarter, Type 4, detached, with garage and storeroom. A three-bedroom house with a sitting room, dining room, kitchen, and a utility room, plus the usual bathroom facilities, this is the level of accommodation that a squadron leader would normally occupy if based at an RAF station.

2

The Missile

The Airframe

The concept of Thor as a single-stage missile with a planned mission profile of 1,500 miles would, at first, seem to be somewhat courageous, especially in the light of the fact that contemporary missiles of this configuration were only achieving ranges in the order of some 250 miles. These missiles were notably the German A-4 design, better known as the much-feared V2 weapon of the Second World War, and its direct descendant, the Redstone missile. Redstone was the product of a group of predominantly V2 scientists brought from Germany as part of Operation Paperclip; they worked under their former wartime colleague, Werner von Braun, at the Redstone Arsenal at Huntsville in Alabama. Even the initial suggestion of an IRBM based on the second stage of the embryonic Titan ICBM would only have an estimated range of 800 miles.

Initial studies into Thor's likely vital statistics—conducted by the US Air Force Ballistic Missile Division—indicated that the missile would need to be in the order of 65 feet long, with a diameter of some 8 feet, and a weight, at launch, of around 55 tons. The results of this study were not revealed to the Douglas Aircraft Company, however, and when asked to go ahead with the design, only certain parameters were specified; this left Douglas to decide the final size and configuration of the vehicle for themselves. The thinking behind this strategy was two-fold. Firstly, if the Douglas design team arrived at essentially the same conclusions as the earlier study, it would provide confirmation of the initial concept. Secondly, in the absence of specific design criteria being insisted upon by the USAF, the contractor could not cite this as a factor if their design came up short. As an intermediate-range ballistic missile could only have any value as a weapon if sited outside of the USA, an essential feature of the design was that it should be capable of being transported by air in the 77-foot (23.5 metres) cargo bay of another Douglas product, the C-124 Globemaster II aircraft.

The design team at Douglas completed their calculations, which proved to be very close indeed to those of the initial USAF study, also believing a single-stage vehicle to be the optimum configuration for the planned mission profile.

Thor would need to possess some innovative features in order to help the designers achieve their objectives. Redstone and the V2 were steered by the use of vanes (a little like a rudder on a boat) placed permanently in the exhaust from the engine thrust chamber, these being moved to deflect the thrust and so achieve a change in direction of the missile. Aerodynamic control surfaces were also provided at the end of the missile fins. This arrangement produced high levels of performance-reducing drag; to overcome this issue, Thor would employ a system by which the thrust chamber of the engine itself moved (gimballed) in order to provide control over the direction of the thrust. Drag reduction, coupled with up-to-date design features and production techniques would all assist Thor to reach the desired range.

Thor's airframe, excluding the nose cone containing the warhead, comprised six basic sections. The forward section, aft of the bulkhead where the nose cone was mated to the missile, was the guidance and control section. Then, in order, came the fuel tank, a short centre body section, the oxidiser tank, another short body section, and finally the engine and accessories compartment.

By far the largest components of the airframe were the fuel and oxidiser tanks. The tanks' design was unusual for the period in which Thor was developed; they were integral sealed portions of the airframe, so that the tank wall was also the skin of the fuselage. This was one of the design features, making a lighter structure that would help to achieve the range that was required. The V2 and Redstone missiles both had an outer skin to the missile and a separate structure for the tanks inside, markedly increasing the overall weight. Thor's tank sections were formed from slabs of high-strength aluminium alloy, measuring 8 feet by 25 feet (2.4 m × 7.6 m). To produce the finished tank section, each slab was stretched, which relieved any internal stresses present and to introduce the required curvature. The US Chemical Milling Corporation chemically milled the panels to produce a 6-mm-thick tank wall with a waffle pattern of integral stiffeners on the inner surface. The chemical milling process removed approximately 10 lb (4.5 kg) of aluminium from each panel and was to a thickness tolerance of 0.003 inches (0.076 mm). Three panels were required to form the complete tank and the long edges of the panels included grooves, used to secure each panel to the adjacent panel. The panels were also welded. Dome-shaped ends (the tanks were pressurised in flight) were bolted and welded to the tank assembly and internal anti-slosh baffles were also included to control the movement of the propellant. The oxidiser tank was of cylindrical section, but the fuel tank was tapered. Fuel tank fill and supply pipe lines passed through the oxidiser tank. A circular vent was provided on the right-hand side of the missile (missile viewed from the rear) at the top of the oxidiser tank section. This was to vent the oxidiser that expanded and changed to gaseous form in the missile while waiting to launch. The vent could be seen billowing white vapour and heard in the form of a roaring sound.

The remaining structural components of the airframe were also of aluminium alloy, but employed a skin and stringer construction. The tanks were joined together

Douglas SM75 THOR

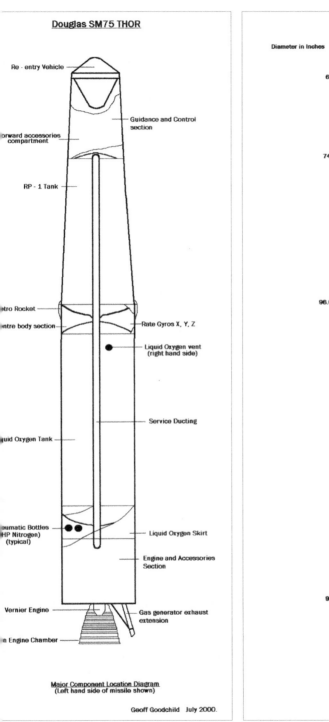

- Re - entry Vehicle
- Guidance and Control section
- orward accessories compartment
- RP - 1 Tank
- etro Rocket
- entre body section
- Rate Gyros X, Y, Z
- Liquid Oxygen vent (right hand side)
- Service Ducting
- quid Oxygen Tank
- eumatic Bottles HP Nitrogen) (typical)
- Liquid Oxygen Skirt
- Engine and Accessories Section
- Vernier Engine
- Gas generator exhaust extension
- n Engine Chamber

Major Component Location Diagram
(Left hand side of missile shown)

Geoff Goodchild   July 2000.

Douglas SM75 THOR

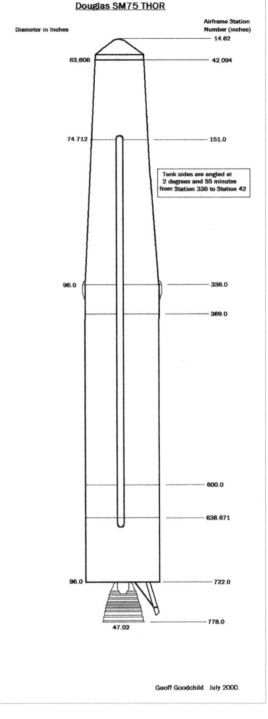

Diameter in Inches

Airframe Station Number (inches)
- 14.62
- 42.094

63.606

74.712 — 151.0

Tank sides are angled at
2 degrees and 55 minutes
from Station 336 to Station 42

96.0 — 336.0
— 369.0

— 600.0
— 636.671

96.0 — 722.0
— 778.0
47.02

Geoff Goodchild   July 2000.

by a short centre body section, which housed the rate gyros (part of the guidance and control system), their access doors, and the two small, solid propellant retro rockets used to facilitate nose cone separation. The retro rockets were diametrically opposed, approximately 25 degrees to the right (top retro) and left (bottom retro) of the centreline respectively, when the missile is viewed from the base. The retro rockets' forward covers were positioned on the tapered tank section.

The guidance and control section above the fuel tank was of monocoque construction, much like an aircraft fuselage, in which the skin absorbs most of the stresses to which the structure is subject. This section continued the tapered shape of the fuel tank and included two large access doors for maintenance of the guidance pallet (the guidance equipment rack) and the guidance ball (the stabilised platform group). The doors were also designed to be stress-bearing structures. The guidance equipment was relatively heavy and the construction of this section included doublers and anchor points, which, together with the circular frames of its basic construction, carried the weight of the stabilised platform group and guidance equipment pallet. Two further, smaller doors were provided in the guidance and control section, the purpose of these being to allow sighting of the guidance platform by the short and long-range theodolites positioned on the launch pad, for guidance alignment prior to launch. A launch umbilical mast, attached to the pad launch mounting, provided the pre-launch countdown routine actions and continuous-use services from the relevant ground-support-equipment components via an interface provided on the right-hand side of the missile, just aft of the nose cone mating point. These services included electrical power, air conditioning, missile and gyro heater monitoring, guidance alignment, and targeting data. At launch, the mast would be rapidly retracted sideways under hydraulic pressure and the service cables would be disconnected by a lanyard attached to the mast.

A further short body section was joined to the bottom of the oxidiser tank. This section was known as the LOX skirt and it provided an attachment point for the rearmost section of the missile—the engine and accessories compartment. The LOX skirt housed four large, spherical pneumatic bottles, which were charged with high-pressure nitrogen gas (GN2) for pressurisation of the fuel tank and other components.

Attached to the aft end of the LOX skirt came the engine and accessories compartment. This section continued the cylindrical cross-section of the missile's lower fuselage and contained the main engine and accessory power systems. The main engine, or sustainer, was mounted through a tripod structure to a triangular set of beams below the oxidiser tank, which in turn transmitted the thrust from the engine to the rest of the vehicle. This structure also supported the vehicle prior to launch. The bottom of the section was enclosed by a base plate, which also provided a location for the small vernier engines. A large central opening allowed the thrust chamber to reach out into the open air. Around the periphery of the missile base plate were six sockets, which were located with the launch pins that held the missile to the launcher. Light alloy assemblies and doubler plates, provided at these locations, spread the weight of the missile onto the support structure. Movement of the missile during fuelling and forces caused by winds (with the missile vertical) caused asymmetric loading at the launch pin locations; this required the sockets to be much stronger than might be imagined, allowing considerable stress to be safely placed on these points. A similar system was provided to spread the stresses imposed by the gimballing of the engine in flight, when the thrust line was not along the missile's axis of symmetry. The section also housed the quick disconnect couplings for the fuel and oxidiser fill lines.

Thor's airframe was originally designed to have four triangular-shaped fins at the base of the engine and accessories section, and indeed, the early prototypes did fly with these aids to stabilisation. On 4 June 1958, Thor no. 115, fitted with the triangular fins, was launched. This was one of the payback launches that Thor performed. Thor had drawn heavily from other programmes and was used when necessary to provide the launch vehicle for testing other missile's systems, hence the term payback. Thor had already been used extensively for testing the Atlas nose cone (as the Thor-able, a modified Thor possessing two stages) and this particular launch was to test the Bell Telephone Laboratories guidance system for the Titan ICBM, which was the next step beyond Atlas and therefore not even near being able to test its own equipment. The object of this exercise was to test the capability of the Titan's guidance system to cope with wind shear. To simulate this possibly violent regime of flight, commands were entered during the initial climb to cause rapid pitching of the missile, which was of sufficient magnitude for it to be seen with the naked eye. During these events, observers reported that they had seen something falling from the Thor. Hearts no doubt stopped for a moment or two in launch control, but, in the cold light of examination, the flight parameters telemetry indicated that the flight profile was proceeding as normal. Search teams had been immediately sent down range to look for the debris and soon recovered a piece of Thor from a swamp. It was one of the triangular-shaped fins. Another fin was found later. The launch, despite the loss of two fins, was a complete success. Engineers had been trying to decide for some time whether the fins on Thor should be deleted, but erred on the side of caution. The loss of the fins had demonstrated that Thor would fly just as well without them. An immediate decision was taken to leave Thors that already had fins to remain so equipped and amend the production line process to delete the fitting of fins. None of the combat-configured Thors were equipped with fins. Another positive aspect of this launch was that the Thor airframe had been convincingly proven to be structurally sound and that really was one less thing to worry about.

As the propellant tanks were integral structures, service lines connecting the equipment bays needed to be routed externally past the tank sections. This was achieved by the provision of fibreglass duct fairings on both sides of the missile.

Thor's airframe principle statistics were as follows: the airframe length from Station 42 (forward bulkhead of guidance section and warhead mating point) was

61 feet 4 inches (18.69 metres)—this included the engine bell. The airframe diameter was 8 feet (2.44 metres); this remained constant until the uppermost edge of the short, inter-tank centre body section, from where it tapered at an angle of 2 degrees and 55 minutes to give a diameter at Station 42 of 5 feet 3.6 inches (1.62 metres). The basic airframe structure, as described above, weighed in at 3,222 lb (1,462 kg).

Pneumatic System

The missile was provided with a pneumatic system, filled with gaseous nitrogen, located in the liquid oxygen skirt, the short body section of the airframe between the engine and accessories compartment, and the LOX tank. The system consisted of four spherical high-pressure storage bottles, their associated interconnecting pipes and controls in the form of valves and pressure switches.

The purpose of the pneumatic system was to pressurise the RP-1 fuel tank, the start tank, the hydraulic fluid tank, and the lubricating oil tank during flight. The system was also used to provide pneumatic pressure for the operation of certain valves and to purge the tanks and engine section before refuelling to reduce fire hazards. It included a feed to the pneumatic control manifold assembly and two quick disconnect couplings, one from the fuel tank pressurisation line and the other being from the nitrogen fill line.

System pressure was maintained by means of a pressure regulator in the missile nitrogen supply, with protection against over-pressurisation provided by a relief valve.

During phase one of the countdown, the pneumatic control manifold assembly on the launch emplacement was pressurised to 135 psi by the hydro-pneumatic systems control trailer firing console. The missile's nitrogen bottles were pressurised to a minimum pressure of 2,850 psi via the nitrogen fill quick disconnect line, which caused the operation of a relay confirming 'missile bottles pressurised' for the countdown sequence.

At the beginning of phase three, nitrogen purging took place, and once the RP-1 fuel tank had received its fuel load, the tank was pre-pressurised; this was achieved from the launch emplacement via the fuel tank pressurisation quick disconnect line. This action also generated a signal for the countdown, but it was carried over to phase five.

During phase five, the final topping off of the LOX tank occurred. With this complete, the LOX tank was pre-pressurised and produced a signal, which, in conjunction with the pre-pressurisation of the fuel tank in phase three, caused operation of a relay in the countdown sequence giving confirmation of 'main tanks pressurised'. Despite the title of the relay's function, the receipt of this signal in the countdown was also dependent upon the start tanks being pressurised.

During the engine start sequence, but before main stage combustion, the missile's fuel tank pressurisation was taken over by the missile's high-pressure bottles.

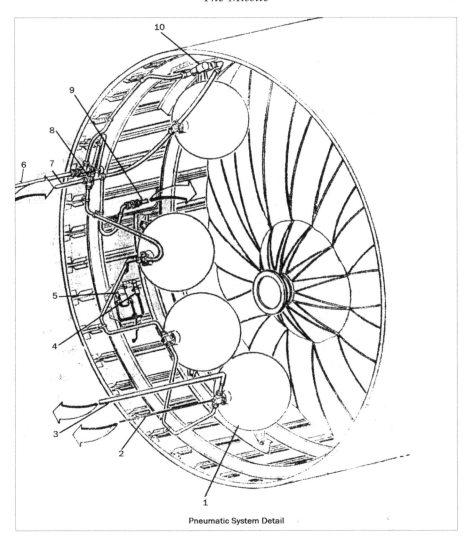

Pneumatic System Detail

Missile nitrogen subsystem. Key to numbered items:
1. High-pressure gas tank (missile bottle).
2. To pressure switch.
3. To pneumatic control manifold assembly.
4. Relief valve.
5. Vent valve (gas dump valve).
6. From fuel tank pressurisation quick disconnect.
7. From nitrogen fill quick disconnect.
8. Check valve.
9. To missile fuel tank.
10. Solenoid valve (missile fuel tank pressurising valve). (*USAF*)

This action was confirmed for the remaining countdown sequence, as was the pressurisation of the lubricating oil tank, and the pressurisation of the LOX tank by gaseous oxygen. At missile lift-off, the quick disconnect couplings would break contact and seal. At the emplacement, the missile's bottle pressurising valves and the pneumatic control manifold assembly valves would be closed.

Fuel System

This section describes Thor's fuel system only to the point at which the fuel and oxidiser supply lines from the tanks meet the turbo pumps, further progression of the fuel and oxidiser being reserved for the description of the engine itself.

Thor's tank walls were those of the airframe itself and it was therefore necessary to route the RP-1 supply pipe through the LOX tank to the engine section of the missile. This clearly had implications for the RP-1, as the freezing point of the fuel was far above the temperature of the LOX, requiring the supply pipe to be insulated and heated. During fuelling, the 6,500-gallon (29,510-litre) LOX tank would always be filled to capacity, but the amount of fuel loaded into the 4,175-gallon (18,954-litre) capacity RP-1 tank was computed by the RP-1 computer, which, as part of its calculations, looked at the density of the fuel and the pressure in the fuel storage tank. The computer was located in a panel on the right-hand side of the electrical equipment trailer.

For phase three, the fuelling phase of the count down, the missile was in the vertical firing position, but it was still attached to its transporter/erector. The clamshell arms were closed tightly around the missile at the point where the guidance section met the top of the fuel tank, prepared to provide some stability against the onslaught about to come. The rate of transfer of propellants to the missile was in the region of 1,800 gallons (8,172 litres) per minute, and for the technicians on the pad, refuelling, especially during early encounters with the process, was quite an experience. The procedure was very noisy and the missile would rock on its launch mount as the heavy load made its way rapidly into the tanks. The author was informed that the initial reaction to run away from the pad soon subsided, however, as experience increased.

On commencement of phase three, the engine and tank sections were purged by nitrogen as a precaution against any fire hazards and the fuelling process began. From the LOX side of the emplacement, the cryogenic liquid was forced through the quick disconnect coupling on the right hand of the missile in rapid flow (a countdown mode) and entered the tank via a mushroom-shaped inlet located at the top. This continued until the LOX tank reached 95 per cent of its capacity, at which point a float switch operated to cause the flow of the oxidiser to cease. Any further LOX flow would now be normally left until phase five—the final phase.

The LOX start tank and the lines to the vernier engines were filled by backpressure during the LOX fill. To achieve this, the LOX tank vent valve was closed. As the start tank filled via the vernier engine bleed valves, vents to the LOX overflow pit on the side of the launch emplacement were opened. The LOX tank vent valve opened again either after the expiration of a 180-second timer or upon a signal indicating that the RP-1 tank had been loaded with 97 per cent of the fuel load.

LOX has a boiling point of –183° Celsius, and once in the missile would begin to boil off and expand back into gaseous oxygen, causing a steady loss of the LOX from the missile's tank. LOX has an expansion ratio of 1:861, which means that a given volume of the liquid would be 861 times that volume as a gas at standard atmospheric pressure at 20° Celsius. The missile was provided with a vent on its right-hand side near the top of the LOX tank, and a cloud of white vapour would be seen issuing from the vent of a LOX-fuelled missile, accompanied by a roaring sound. The loss of LOX imposed a time limit on how long a Thor could be held on the launch pad after fuelling. This time was variable as it was dependent upon other factors, such as the wind speed—given by an anemometer positioned on a post near to or on the launch control trailer—outside air temperature, and humidity. The values of these factors were written on the missiles status board. By entering these parameters onto a nomograph, which is a graphical calculating device, the maximum hold time could be determined. Although the RP-1 supply pipe was insulated and heated, there were some issues for the fuel in a prolonged hold.

The LOX tank wall would be super cooled by its contents and this would cause the outside air in contact with the surface of the missile to be cooled below its dew point and to condense out and then freeze. The LOX tank section of the missile would therefore be covered in a layer of ice. Video footage of missiles using LOX as an oxidiser will show ice being shed from the region of the LOX tank during the launch.

From the opposite side of the launch emplacement, RP-1 would be roaring through its dedicated quick disconnect coupling on its way into the upper tank of the missile, entering via a mushroom-shaped inlet at the top of the tank. The fuel tank vent valve was open in order to avoid a build-up of backpressure as Thor received her fuel.

RP-1 entered the missile through a flow meter counter in rapid flow until 97 per cent of the computed fuel load was on board, thereafter switching to fine flow to complete the fuel loading to 100 per cent at a less frenetic pace. Once fuelling had been completed, the fuel tank vent valve was closed. The RP-1 tank was pre-pressurised with gaseous nitrogen during phase five of the countdown.

Generally, practice countdowns that involved propellant loading were confined to loading the LOX into the missile. On occasion, there would be a call for a dual propellant flow exercise, requiring the flow of both LOX and RP-1. It should be noted that, for this exercise, the RP-1 was not loaded into the missile; the fuel supply pipe from the storage tank was connected to a flexible hose at the RP-1 valve complex one (missile end of the supply pipe) and routed into a mobile tanker brought onto the pad for this purpose. This ensured safety in that there could be no accidental launch, however unlikely that may have been, and was to avoid the need for subsequent specialist cleaning of the missile fuel tank, a process that was not available in the UK.

Although a good deal of the countdown was electronically monitored, progress being signalled by various lights and captions, there were required elements that had no such confirmation. Certain valves changing position, for example, while vital to the countdown, were not subject to their operation being remotely verified. Technicians on the pad would therefore revert to more basic, but highly effective, almost infallible methods. They would simply listen via a headset to the confirmatory noises from Thor's inner workings, much in the same way as a doctor might listen to a patient's chest.

It was noted earlier that, during phase three, a float switch in the LOX tank operated as the contents reached 95 per cent of capacity, causing the flow of LOX to cease, resuming once again in phase five of the countdown. During the period of time between the initial LOX fill and the commencement of phase five, the LOX had been boiling off, expanding through the missile vent as gaseous oxygen, and depleting the LOX tank contents. As the phase five 'begin signal' was received, the flow of LOX into the missile would resume in rapid load until the 95 per cent switch operated for the second time. This time, the flow did not cease, but the LOX tank vent valve closed and the LOX tank-pressurising valve opened. A relay operated as 99 per cent LOX capacity was reached and the LOX flow switched to fine load until the tank contents reached 100 per cent capacity. This signalled all LOX loading valves to close. The LOX tank was pre-pressurised with gaseous nitrogen. After engine start, pressurisation of the LOX tank would be via gaseous oxygen formed by passing liquid oxygen from the main propellant supply through a heat exchanger in the gas generator exhaust extension.

At launch on a typical mission profile, the propellants aboard the missile would account for some 98,000 lb (44,464 kg) of the missile's mass.

Engine

Thor had been designed to draw, wherever possible, on technology already in existence or currently being developed. The propulsion system was no exception.

The engine for Thor was based on a unit previously designed for the North American Aviation Navaho intercontinental cruise missile. The original engine, developed by North American Aviation's Rocketdyne division, was a two-chambered liquid propellant rocket engine used as a booster to launch and then accelerate the aircraft-like missile to supersonic speed, from where its main ram jet engines would take over. The Navaho was cancelled during 1957 in favour of the development programme for the ICBM, the first of which was to be the Convair Atlas. Navaho's booster design, however, was destined to live on, modified to a single-chamber engine and due to serve as a booster for Atlas, which would utilise two such units. As the requirement for Thor emerged, it was suggested that the project should borrow a 'half Atlas booster', the single unit serving as the missile's main engine. On Atlas, the boosters, each of 165,000-lb thrust, were jettisoned on achieving a certain phase in the flight profile, resulting in a relatively short burn time. In the role of a main engine, the burn time could be expected to increase, and therefore, to ensure the longevity of the engine, the thrust was derated to 150,000 lb for use in Thor. In addition to this, Thor also borrowed two small LR-101-NA-11 vernier engines, each of 1,000 lb thrust, which, while adding to the overall thrust available in the other axes, would also provide roll control and fine tuning of the missile's velocity prior to warhead separation.

Rocketdyne designated the Thor engine the LR-79 (USAF designation LR-79-NA-9). The 'LR' designation describes the type of engine, in this case a liquid-fuelled rocket engine, and the '79' is simply the next number in sequence of engine design. There was a convention, now unused, that odd numbers were allocated to Air Force engines and even numbers allocated to those for the Navy. A designation preceded by an 'X' indicates an experimental engine. Due to the design work on Atlas already in progress and some early decisions, such as how the LOX and RP-1 feed would mate with the missile, Rocketdyne were enjoying a head start. This allowed a mock-up of the engine to be delivered to Douglas in February 1956, something of an achievement. In fact, the engine was the most important part of the sub-systems for the missile at this stage because the missile would be designed around it. A very useful value to have in the design stage of an engine is the specific impulse (usually abbreviated to 'Isp'), which is a way of describing the efficiency of a rocket engine. It represents the thrust developed with respect to the amount of propellant used per unit time. The higher the value of the specific impulse, the more thrust is produced for the same amount of propellant. If the propellant used is given in terms of weight (the mass of the propellant with due allowance for gravity), then specific impulse is stated in units of time (i.e. seconds). The design weight of a missile will define the value of thrust that will be required. Dividing the thrust required by the specific impulse, which was determined as a result of thermodynamic analysis, will yield the weight flow of propellants the engine must produce. The very important issue here is that this information determines the physical size of the engine. The Isp of the LR-79 was 285s—higher than that of the V2 and Redstone and another of the measures designed to assist in achieving Thor's required range.

Engine development continued apace. The first experimental XLR-79 delivered to Douglas for airframe mated firing tests was during June 1956. Development work on the engine was undertaken at Rocketdyne's facility at Canoga Park, California, while actual production would take place in Neosho, Missouri, with delivery of the engines scheduled to commence in July 1957. Static test firings were conducted at three Californian sites—Santa Susana, Edwards Air Force Base, and the Douglas facility in Sacremento.

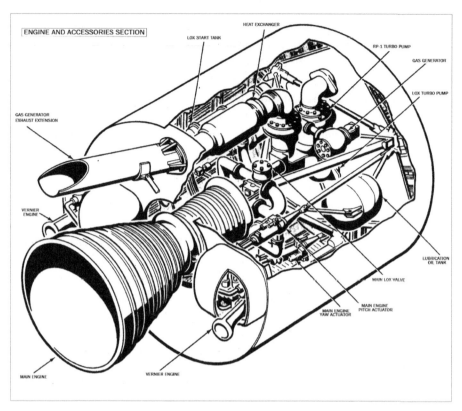

Major engine components were mounted in a tripod-like upper structure of welded steel tubes, which also transmitted the engine's thrust to the missile airframe via a set of triangular beams below the liquid oxygen tank. Initially, the attachments to the beams were by rigid ball and socket fixings, but anti-vibration mountings were soon considered for production Thors.

Below this section of the engine was the gimbal-mounted thrust chamber, which would direct the thrust of the engine as dictated by the flight control system. The actuators that controlled the chamber in its axes of freedom, pitch, and yaw were themselves anchored at one end on the upper structure. The bottom of the engine and accessories section was enclosed by a base plate, which also provided the mountings for the small vernier engines. A central opening accommodated the passage of the thrust chamber into the open air.

The fuel and oxidiser tanks were pressurised in order to maintain a positive head of pressure for delivery of the propellants to the turbopumps. Turbopumps were required to deliver fuel to the combustion chamber at the correct flow rate and pressure. It would not be possible to simply use tank pressurisation for this as the pressures required would be extremely high, consequently requiring the propellant and pressurising tanks to be of prohibitively heavy construction. Use of a lightweight turbopump permitted the tanks' construction to be of very low

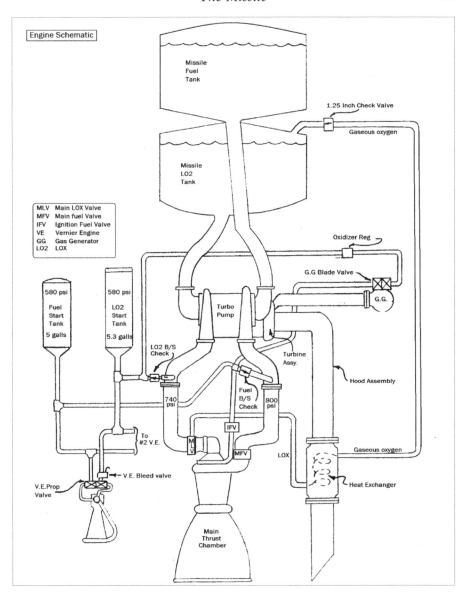

Engine Schematic

Missile Fuel Tank

1.25 Inch Check Valve

Gaseous oxygen

Missile LO2 Tank

MLV	Main LOX Valve
MFV	Main fuel Valve
IFV	Ignition Fuel Valve
VE	Vernier Engine
GG	Gas Generator
LO2	LOX

Oxidizer Reg

G.G Blade Valve

580 psi

Fuel Start Tank

5 galls

580 psi

LO2 Start Tank

5.3 galls

Turbo Pump

G.G.

LO2 B/S Check

Turbine Assy.

Hood Assembly

740 psi

Fuel B/S Check

800 psi

IFV

To #2 V.E.

M L V

Gaseous oxygen

MFV

LOX

Heat Exchanger

V.E. Bleed valve

V.E.Prop Valve

Main Thrust Chamber

mass and pressurised at a practical low pressure. The RP-1 fuel tank was pressurised by gaseous nitrogen at 60 psi via a pressure-reducing valve, supplied from the four high-pressure nitrogen bottles in the LOX skirt of the missile; the LOX tank was pre-pressurised by gaseous nitrogen prior to engine start, but thereafter by gaseous oxygen generated by passing LOX through a heat exchanger in the gas generator exhaust.

From the tanks, the fuel and oxidiser were routed to the turbopump assembly. The turbopumps consisted of two large centrifugal pumps (impellers) driven by a high-speed, single-stage turbine through a reduction gearbox. Centrifugal type turbopumps, although larger than the axial flow type, especially for low-density fluids, were much more powerful. The turbine developed in excess of 2,500 hp, being driven by the gas generator, a spherical combustion chamber fuelled by the same propellants as the engine. The propellants for starting the gas generator were drawn from the start tanks and electrically ignited during the engine start sequence.

Referring to the photograph of the XLR-79 engine, the dark-coloured spherical gas generator combustion chamber will be seen with, above, the turbine, to the right of which is the very large turbopump assembly. Also evident in the photograph is the tripod-like support structure.

The hot gases developed by the gas generator were routed to the turbine, across which they expanded, causing a rotational speed of approximately 31,000 rpm. The reduction gearbox in the turbopump assembly reduced this speed at a ratio of 4.8:1, giving the turbopumps a rotational speed of some 6,400 rpm. The turbine in the photograph is shown without its hood and exhaust assembly, which, when fitted, incorporates the LOX heat exchanger and extends through the base plate of the missile next to the main engine thrust chamber. In order to keep within the temperature limits of the turbine blades, the gas generator required an excess of RP-1 fuel that, when exhausted from the gas generator exhaust extension at the base of the missile, could be seen burning off in the form of the irregular pulsing flame that is so characteristic of a Thor launch.

There were some initial problems with the blades of the gas generator turbine. At the high rotational speeds of their operation, the blade tips began to flutter, causing fatigue at the root (hub) of the blade. This resulted in the cracking, and in some cases breaking, of the blade. The solution to this problem was readily available and the blade tips were fitted with shrouds, which extended from the tip of one blade over the tip of its neighbour. The blades were still free to move around slightly, as they must, but just enough damping was provided to cure the flutter. It is interesting to note that due to the pace at which the Thor programme had to proceed, even a broken turbine blade was not allowed to slow up the progress. If a blade, or blades, fractured, any faulty blade was removed along with the blade that was diametrically opposed; this was done in order to restore symmetry and allow the testing to continue. In this way, a relatively simple problem did not bring down the whole test programme.

The photograph of the turbopump assembly shows the very prominent propellant inlet flanges. The inlet on the left in this view is the RP-1 inlet, while that on the right is for the LOX. The thinner, annular parts of the assembly house the impellers. It can be seen that the propellants are fed through the vanes in the inlets, through the elbow, and into the middle of the impeller for onward transmission to the thrust chamber. The lubricating oil system for the turbopumps was a 'total loss' system; oil that had passed through the turbopumps was then discharged overboard. The oil was provided from the lubricating oil tank, the spherical-looking grey coloured object below the LOX flange in the photograph, and was kept positively pressurised by gaseous nitrogen. Used oil was discharged near to and burned off in the turbo pump exhaust. The turbopumps passed propellants to the thrust chamber at a rate of 450 lb per second for the LOX and 200 lb per second for the RP-1. This equates to a LOX to RP-1 ratio of 2.25:1. The pressure in the LOX feed to the thrust chamber was 740 psi, while the RP-1 feed was at 800 psi.

During research and development, engines were test fired and then stripped and carefully examined in a bid to discover if any problems were evident. Any issues so raised could be addressed in the form of modifications to later engines. One such post-firing examination early in 1957 had revealed that the turbopump bearings might be moving axially in their mountings. Although there had been no evidence of this being an issue in flight testing, the ballistic missile division requested that Rocketdyne investigate the matter with a view to eliminating this bearing-walking.

Flight testing continued, and on 11 October 1957, Thor 108 soared away from its pad and out over the ocean. The missile performed well in all respects until just a few moments before the planned main engine cut-off (MECO) point, when the engine stopped. The Thor fell a little short of its mission profile distance, but it was so close to MECO when it shut down that it was considered to be a very, very minor malfunction. Some six months later, however, the ghost of Thor 108 would return to haunt the flight test team.

Thor 116 lifted from its pad on 23 April 1958, but 146 seconds into the powered flight phase, propulsion of the missile ceased. Examination of the telemetry indicated that the cause of the premature engine shut down was turbopump gearbox failure. Thoughts turned back to Thor 108, the data was recalled and examined in detail. There it was, evidence of turbopump gearbox failure, the first manifestation of this issue in flight.

The problem now was whether to cancel some upcoming missions (some involving the moon) or to go ahead and hope that all would be well. The decision was that the gearboxes seemed to have a failure rate of about one in seven, having suffered two failures in fourteen launches, and so the flight tests were scheduled to continue with the calculated risk of further failure, which, unfortunately, did occur. Generally, the required service life of a turbopump is one to two hours, although modern designs tend to give about a factor of ten on this.

Beyond the turbopumps, at the bottom end of the thrust frame, came the main gimbal—the attachment point of the thrust chamber. The chamber at the gimbal end was of a basically cylindrical section, which converged slightly to form a throat. The primary combustion took place in this area, where temperature and pressure reached 3,150° Celsius (5,700° Fahrenheit) and 550 psi respectively. From the throat, the chamber opened out into the easily recognised bell-shaped nozzle. As the gases flowed through the throat into the divergent main nozzle, they underwent laminar cooling, which absorbed very large amounts of the generated heat.

Bell-shaped nozzles have proved to have very good performance while allowing the nozzles to be relatively short. The bell on the LR-79 was 56 inches (1.42 metres) in length, with a final diameter of 47.02 inches (1.19 metres). The bell type of design works by providing a rapid expansion or radial flow section in the initial divergent region of the nozzle. This leads to a uniform, axial flow at the nozzle exit. The interior concave contour of the bell is changed gradually so that oblique shockwaves are not encouraged to form.

The thrust chamber was constructed from over 300 heat-resistant nickel-alloy tubes of nominally 0.45 inch (11.43 mm) diameter. They went through a process to impart a basically rectangular section, which tapered from a maximum at the open end of the engine bell to the minimum at the throat. For the formation of the chamber, a vertical jig, which conformed precisely to the interior profile of the engine bell, was utilised. The preformed tubes were positioned around the jig and once all were in place, seamless steel bands were placed over the bell. Each tube was carefully brazed to the next with silver solder, while the seamless steel bands were welded to the structure. The spacing of the steel bands essentially reflected the pressure exerted at that point of the bell in normal operation. The bands can be seen in the gap between the protective red shells covering the bell in the photograph of the complete engine. Along the length of the divergent bell section, the bands are quite widely spaced, but around the throat and the primary combustion area, visible immediately forward of the protective shells, they are close enough together to be considered a continuous jacket. Also of note in this view are the cylindrical start tanks at the top left of the engine.

With this process complete, the injector plate, a large, high-strength steel forging was fitted, through which the fuel and oxidiser flowed into the chamber. X-ray and hydrostatic checks were carried out to check the structural integrity and to search for leaks between tubes. With the engine in operation, RP-1 flowed through the tubes that made up the chamber to assist in keeping the temperature of the chamber walls to an acceptable level, in a process known as regenerative cooling.

The photograph of the interior of the chamber clearly shows the cylindrical primary combustion area, the throat, and the individual tubes that make up the chamber. The silver-coloured injector plate and its holes for delivering the propellants can be seen at the head of the chamber. The propellants in the chamber were ignited electrically, the igniter being screwed into the centre of the injector plate. The approved technique for inserting the igniter was by using a long rod with the igniter gripped at its end. Trying to hit a small threaded hole with the end of a long, somewhat unstable rod in poor light seemed, for some reason, to create a certain amount of tension in those charged with executing this task. One technician reported to the author that he developed a technique, which involved inserting a spreader device into the thrust chamber and by very, very, carefully lying down on it, the igniter could be inserted by hand. While the unofficial technique no doubt saved time and possibly temper, it must still have been a stressful exercise until exiting the chamber with the bell tubes intact. By referring back to the first photograph in this chapter, it will be seen that the injector plate is clearly visible on the left of the photograph, bolted solidly to the top of the combustion chamber.

Every engine was hot tested (fired) at Neosho. A normal test would last from fifteen to thirty seconds. Each engine was further tested to check the gimballing pivot and to calculate the moment of inertia of the chamber and its precise geometric centre, with these factors influencing the accuracy of the missile's guidance. The thrust chamber provided for control of the missile's flight path in two axes, pitch and yaw, and could be gimballed up to 7 degrees in each axis.

The two small 1,000-lb thrust LR-101 vernier engines, which also operated to assist in pitch and yaw, provided the sole means of flight path control in roll.

After MECO, the verniers would operate alone to impart a fine tuning of the missile's final velocity and positioning prior to payload separation. The verniers were small rocket motors, mounted diametrically opposed on the missile base plate. They were positioned 90 degrees away from the gas generator exhaust extension, which marks the top surface of the missile. The vernier combustion chambers consisted of an inner and an outer element, both made from steel. Once produced, the outer casing was split along its length and welded back together to encase the inner element of the chamber, the resulting gap between the two structures being utilised for regenerative cooling by RP-1, which, through a helix arrangement in the gap, had a spiral flow pattern imparted to it. The chambers were supported by a light alloy assembly, which allowed the verniers to move in two axes. Hydraulic actuators, commanded by the flight control system, exercised control over the verniers by means of a rack and pinion in each axis. The vernier engines had a freedom of movement of up to 45 degrees in the pitch axis with a maximum of 34 degrees to outboard in the yaw axis.

The LR-79 and the two LR-101 verniers together formed the MB-3, which is the usual nomenclature for the Thor propulsion group. The propulsion system weighed 2,324 lb (1,054 kg), with a total thrust (including verniers) of 152,000 lb.

The engine, along with most things Thor, evolved as time and technology progressed. The early engines, an experimental example of which features in the photographs accompanying this text, boasted forty-six major components. In later models, this number had been reduced to twenty-eight. This was largely due to a simplified starting and control system, which provided a miniaturised control panel and eliminated the need for the start tanks

As might be expected, the engine start sequence completed phase five, the last stage of the countdown. When all other countdown requirements were satisfied, the igniters for both vernier engines and the main engine fired. The main LOX valve at the thrust chamber opened, as did the ignition fuel valve. The main chamber pilot ignited in a LOX-rich mixture. As this was occurring, the gas generator igniters fired, the vernier engine propellant valves opened, and the verniers lit and were now running. The gas generator blade valves opened and the gas generator was fed with propellants, itself achieving combustion and causing the turbine and, in turn, the turbopumps to rapidly spin up. The main fuel valve opened, and with the propellant flow now at the correct ratios, thrust chamber combustion took place. Full thrust was developed very rapidly and the missile lifted from the pad.

Hydraulic System

The purpose of the missile hydraulic system was to provide hydraulic pressure to the thrust chamber actuators of the main sustainer and vernier engines to enable pitch, roll, and yaw control of the missile during flight.

The hydraulic pump, powered by the accessory drive pad on the turbo pump gear box, supplied hydraulic fluid under pressure to servo valves and hydraulic pistons that gimballed the sustainer engine and vernier thrust chambers as commanded by the flight control system. Feedback transducers, which were physically connected to the hydraulic actuators, sensed the amount of thrust chamber movement away from its null position and fed back a cancellation signal to the flight control system.

The other main components of the hydraulic system comprised the fluid reservoir, a relief valve, and a system accumulator. Thor's hydraulic system required a special fluid for its operation. The reservoir, or tank, was pressurised by gaseous nitrogen to ensure a positive head of pressure, in order to prevent system cavitation; this occurs when there is a discontinuity in the hydraulic fluid, and it may lead to the formation of bubbles. This has a detrimental effect on hydraulic pumps and can also lead to overheating, as any trapped air in the fluid that has formed into bubbles will generate heat as it is compressed.

The accumulator, also pressurised by gaseous nitrogen, was present to prevent momentary pressure drops in the event that system demand exceeded pump capacity and also to absorb any shocks caused by sudden changes in system pressure. Compressibility of the nitrogen allowed the accumulator to absorb and smooth out any pressure ripples caused by pump operation and the changes in pressure caused by the operation of system components such as jacks and valves. It also served to maintain system pressure, up to the limit of its piston movement, when the pump ceased operation. The accumulator pressure gauge was positioned behind an inspection flap on the left-hand side of the missile engine and accessories compartment.

There were two hydraulic actuators mounted on each of the engines to facilitate the gimballing of the thrust chambers. The hydraulic actuators consisted of a hydraulic controller and a linear-motor feedback transducer, this being a component that measures one type of energy action and feeds the measured quantity back to a device controlling the signal for comparison. The controller components were an electro-hydraulic servo valve and the actuator.

The purpose of the actuators was simply to convert hydraulic energy into mechanical motion of the thrust chambers. In the case of the sustainer engine, one end of each actuator was anchored to the structure of the missile, while the piston rods at the other end of the actuators were connected to lever arm linkages on the thrust chamber itself, which translated the piston movement into movement of the thrust chamber. The design of the actuators allowed for operating loads in the region of 1,000 lb (454 kg). Despite the heavy loads, the design of the hydraulic system necessarily enabled very fine movement of the thrust chamber. The actuators for the vernier engines consisted of two single-ended pistons connected by a rack. In operation, the movement of the rack turned a pinion gear on a shaft, which in turn rotated the vernier engine thrust chambers.

The actuators on the sustainer engine provided for pitch and yaw control, one actuator being dedicated to each control function. The vernier engines were each provided with a yaw actuator and an actuator that combined the pitch and roll functions, dependent upon the signals received from the flight control system. In this latter case, if the verniers operated synchronously, then the resultant control function would be pitch; however, if they were signalled to operate in opposite directions, then the resultant control function would be roll.

The hydraulic servo valves controlled the flow of hydraulic fluid to the actuators, proportional to the signal received from the filter-servo amplifiers of the flight control system. A servo-amplifier is an electronic device that amplifies and converts an alternating current electrical input signal to direct current output to activate electro-hydraulic servo-valves. The direction of valve motion was controlled by the direction of the net current flow in the valve coil. The servo valves provided precise control of the position of the thrust chambers.

Provision was made for the missile's hydraulic system to be pressurised by the ground support equipment prior to the missile's hydraulic pump becoming available. This pressure was provided by the hydro-pneumatic systems control trailer (HPT) and took place in phase one of the countdown to centre the engine thrust chambers. A period of about ten seconds was required for the system to reach working pressure. During phase two of the countdown, the engine thrust chambers were slewed as a system check. Once this was completed, the hydraulic elements of phase two would continue.

Electrical System

Thor's electrical system, located in the forward accessories compartment, consisted of a battery, inverter, power-changeover switch, and associated wiring harnesses and cabling. It distributed AC and DC electrical power supplies to the missile systems during the countdown and in flight.

The source of DC power during flight and in the latter stages of the launch countdown was the missile battery, which provided 28V DC and was kept trickle charged from a missile battery charger panel in the EET.

Missile AC power was produced by a motor-driven inverter, which included voltage and frequency regulators. An inverter is an electrical power converter that changes direct current (DC) to alternating current (AC); the converted AC can be at any required voltage and frequency with the use of appropriate transformers, switching, and control circuits. The input to Thor's inverter was 28V DC from the missile battery and its output provided the 115V AC, 400 Hz, three-phase power necessary for the operation of the guidance system and the control and electronics assembly (CEA).

During the early stages of the launch countdown, all elements of the electrical supplies to the missile were provided from the electrical equipment trailer (EET). As phase one commenced, the ground support equipment 28V DC supply was energised. The missile's inverter power supply panel was powered and readied for operation in phase four of the countdown. The missile's power converter now converted its 120V 60-Hz input supply to 115V 400-Hz three-phase power for operation of the CEA and equipment warm up.

As the countdown progressed, the missile systems were progressively transferred to internal power. At the commencement of phase four, a fifteen-second time delay was energised, which would allow confirmation that the missile inverter was powered and up to speed, producing a steady supply voltage and frequency. If the inverter output was within limits, the missile inverter would take over the task of supplying the CEA. This would be achieved by break-before-make switching. The missile would be disconnected from the missile power converter and, a few milliseconds later, the supply from the inverter would be connected to the loads. This provided a smooth transition to the missile's internal electrical system power, as connecting the missile's inverter to the system before disconnecting the missile's power converter would require that these AC sources be synchronised. The paralleling of non-synchronised AC sources had the potential to cause great damage to the systems involved.

As phase four continued, the missile's battery trickle charger was disconnected from the battery and the missile's battery was connected to the loads it would supply in flight. This would be achieved by make-before-break switching, in which the battery was connected to its loads before the ground support equipment 28V DC power was disconnected. There were no issues with the paralleling of DC sources as there were with AC.

With these actions complete, the battery was supplying all DC loads on the missile, including the missile's inverter, which was producing the required AC power. The missile was now, electrically, independent and ready for flight.

The re-entry vehicle was provided with its own dedicated battery and circuitry and is described in a later section.

The electrical system weighed 411 lb (186.5 kgs).

Guidance

Introduction

The purpose of a ballistic missile system is to carry the re-entry vehicle containing the payload to a point in space from which it can be released and then, travelling in free fall under the influence of the gravitational pull of the Earth, follow a flight path to the correct target.

Once the re-entry vehicle is released in space and commences this unpowered, unguided phase of its flight, it follows a true ballistic trajectory—it travels from its release point to the target in the same way that an artillery shell (a true missile) will travel to its target from the muzzle of a gun.

If a missile such as Thor could be aimed at the correct angle, both in pitch and azimuth, and could achieve its maximum velocity at the very moment of launch, it would behave exactly as a shell leaving a gun and it would be possible to simply fire the missile at the intended target. However, this is not possible due to the fundamental differences between the launching of a ballistic missile and the firing of a shell. Firstly, the missile does not possess an instantaneous velocity and so, at the moment of launch, its velocity is zero; further, as the missile rises on launch, its speed will build up only relatively gradually as the resistance to its forward motion produced by the atmosphere and the force of gravity are overcome. The force of gravity will act upon the missile throughout its flight. Initially, it may appear that this would be a constant factor for which a relatively simple allowance could be made, but, in reality, gravity varies from place to place on the Earth's surface and it will also vary with the height of the missile above the ground. The second problem is that this type of missile is usually much too large to consider launching from anything other than the vertical position. Therefore, the missile will need to be steered onto the desired path in space, following a powered ballistic trajectory, which will require the provision of some form of control system within the missile.

Returning to consider the trajectory of a shell for a moment longer, a shell fired from a gun located on a perfectly spherical planet that possessed no atmosphere would describe a flight path that, in terms of altitude reached, speed, and time, would be perfectly symmetrical. The Earth, however, is not spherical and it does possess an atmosphere, one that is in a constant state of change. Therefore, due allowance must be made for the effects upon the flight path of various factors, which include the density of the atmosphere, the effects of and differences in the force of gravity, and the rotation and the shape of the Earth. Further allowances are required in order to cater for the difference in height of the firing point and the target and also for the wind. Despite the seeming complexity, accurate allowances can be calculated. However, once the shell has been fired, nothing can be changed and there will be only one flight path that it can possibly follow.

The flight path of a missile is also affected by these same properties of the planet and its atmosphere. If the properties of the Earth's atmosphere could always be precisely anticipated and if it were possible for all missiles of a given type to be absolutely identical in every respect, the control system would only need to be in the form of an extremely simple autopilot. The missile's position and velocity could be precisely pre-calculated and a trajectory programmed, the separation of the re-entry vehicle occurring at a given time. However, even with the tight manufacturing tolerances that can be achieved today, it would not be possible to ensure that each and every missile of a particular type was identical in every respect. Differences, however slight, in terms of mass, aerodynamics, and thrust developed, would be a certainty and performance would, inevitably, vary between missiles; these differences combined to translate into differences in the trajectories achieved. As the position of a missile is a function of its velocity, the position of a given missile would not be predictable as it would not necessarily achieve the pre-calculated velocities at any given point on its trajectory. Additionally, consideration has to be given to the velocity of the Earth's rotation at the launch point. If the velocity of a missile were not as pre-calculated then its flight time would be different to that planned, and this variation alone would result in an east–west target error. The other major factor is that the atmosphere is in a continuous state of change and, although the automatic pilot would hold the correct heading and pitch angle of the missile, any factor (such as variation in wind velocity) resulting in the lateral displacement of the missile from its pre-calculated trajectory would not be detected, resulting in further targeting errors. Therefore, in our far from ideal world, a much greater degree of sophistication is required for accurately navigating the missile onto the correct trajectory, and compensation for these variable factors is achieved by the provision of a guidance system.

When the USAF began to develop the ICBM, the secret base of operations for those involved was an old parochial school building in Inglewood, California. No uniforms were worn, and to the casual observer, suited businessmen with briefcases came and went. There was nothing to advertise that this was the centre of activity surrounding the development of the future United States strategic missile force. In this single-storey building, preliminary design work on the Atlas ICBM was proceeding apace with a small team, set up along speciality component lines, of senior USAF officers each representing his own particular specialty and leading his own group. Thus there was a propulsion group, an airframe group, and a guidance and control group, the latter being under the command of Colonel (later Dr) B. Paul Blasingame.

None of the team could have guessed that long before Atlas became a reality, they would be instrumental in producing the Thor IRBM. When the Thor project came into existence, work already completed on the Atlas included the main engines (North American Aviation's Rocketdyne division) and a study and experimental work on an inertial guidance system in Dr Charles Stark Draper's laboratory at the Department of Aeronautics of the Massachusetts Institute of Technology (MIT). Technical support during the development work was to be provided by the newly formed Ramo-Wooldridge Corporation, under contract to the Western Development Division, directed by General Bernard Schriever. The Ramo-Wooldridge technical staff, who were electronic specialists, argued for Thor to be equipped with a radar guidance system that employed a ground-based radar with a transponder in the missile (both adapted from the Nike air defence missile) and a ground-based digital computer. This system was under development by Bell Telephone Laboratories.

Colonel Paul Blasingame's guidance and control group, however, were very keen to employ an all-inertial guidance system, which offered the substantial military advantage that once launched, the missile is autonomous. Unlike missiles that relied on external links, such as radar or radio command guidance, while in flight (as in the Ramo-Wooldridge proposal for Thor and that provided for the later Titan I), Thor would not be subject to the dangers of external interference, either accidental or intentional. Loss of signal due to atmospheric activity would not be of concern, and as there was no requirement to transmit its position back to the ground-based elements of a radio or radar system, the missile did not actively advertise its presence to an enemy. With an all-inertial system, every aspect of Thor's guidance in flight would be measured, computed, and executed on board.

There followed several months of study and intense debate between the groups, the outcome being the decision to develop the two possible guidance systems for Thor. Still very much favouring the inertial system, tests of the equipment in static, rocket-sled, and non-ballistic flight tests persuaded the USAF not to proceed with the radar guidance system even before the first inertially guided Thor flight had taken place, and the all-inertial system was adopted for the operational Thor weapon system. The radar system was put to good use, ultimately, in the role of missile test range instrumentation.

Perhaps surprisingly, inertial guidance is actually quite simple in its basic principles. The really difficult part was the engineering of the precision components to the exacting tolerances required to achieve the degree of accuracy necessary for ballistic missile operations. Alongside that came the need for the computing capability to turn the measured data into a viable guidance solution and it was largely for these reasons that inertial systems did not appear at a much earlier stage, another very important factor being that the cost of developing such systems was astronomical. The cost factor in this case had simply to be borne as these systems were now required for defence purposes; this also ensured that development was somewhat more rapid than might otherwise have been expected.

The AC Spark Plug company, (ACSP), despite its name, had a long history of developing and manufacturing automatic pilots, fire control and bombing systems, and other precision military hardware. While working on a fire control system in association with MIT, the company developed an interest in the work being conducted on inertial guidance by the institute's Dr Charles Stark Draper and Dr Walter Wrigley. During 1951, ACSP began to develop a stellar inertial bombing system (SIBS) for the USAF. At that time, it was believed that all-inertial equipment would not provide sufficient accuracy alone and that celestial fixes (hence the stellar) would be required to supplement the inertial equipment for accurate position fixing. The system was large, weighing in at some 5,000 lb (2,268 kg). The SIBS was fitted and flown in a Boeing B-50 bomber (a larger engined, larger tailed version of the B-29 Superfortress) commanded for the test flights by Captain (later Lt-Gen.) Abner Martin. The ACSP engineer on the flights was Paul O. Larson, destined to become the chief engineer of the entire Thor guidance system.

Ironically, the star tracker tasked with the celestial fixes did not perform that well, but the inertial guidance element alone was very successful, achieving accuracies in the order of 1 mile per hour (positional accuracy).

With the decision to opt for inertial guidance, the previous successes of the SIBS flight tests held ACSP in good stead and, based on those results, the company was awarded the contract for the Thor guidance system. The system developed for Thor was the all-inertial AC Achiever, a version of which was already in use on the US Navy Regulus II cruise missile.

As the Thor programme gained momentum, AC Spark Plug transferred all of its inertial guidance production from its plants at Milwaukee, Wisconsin, on the western shores of Lake Michigan, to a new facility, owned by General Motors, ACSP's parent company, in nearby Oak Creek, just 11 miles to the south. The specialised tooling and equipment required was government financed on a special tooling contract.

The production tolerances required were quite extraordinary, particularly when considering that this was the 1950s. An example here is that the taper of a particular gyro wheel must not exceed 1/20,000 of an inch and the mass shift of the gyro wheel on its bearings must not exceed one millionth of an inch.

Every part of the gyros had to be thoroughly deburred, as a single particle of a diameter as little as two microns could render the gyro's performance as useless for the task. Originally, liquid honing and sand blasting were the techniques used in this process, when possible, but efforts were always in progress to develop more sophisticated methods. After this process, the parts were examined extensively under a 30× power microscope. Any further cleaning required was then painstakingly carried out by manual means, with an unlikely sounding array of specialist tools, which included dental tools, rubber erasers, steel wool, and sewing needles that were specially ground to form tool shapes

The Thor programme often held surprises and perhaps another is that approximately 70 per cent of the personnel working on the inertial system were women and girls with no previous industrial type experience. It was not unusual for a girl to spend several hours deburring a single gyro component in order to achieve the required standard. The male personnel were engaged on supervisory duties, setting up the machine tools, and the heavier operations.

The gyros were assembled in clean rooms that were supplied with air conditioned and filtered air under pressure to keep foreign matter away, and were also strictly temperature controlled. In addition to this, the rooms were vacuum cleaned and washed down twice each day. Each tool set was used on one gyro only, before being packed and sent for cleaning. This prevented a contaminated tool from ruining more than one gyro. Once cleaned, the tools were repackaged in airtight bags and returned for use in the assembly rooms. The cleanliness regime naturally extended to the workforce. Everyone working on the system wore smocks and hats and those involved in gyro assembly were required to use a specially formulated hand lotion that closed off the skin pores. The girls were not permitted to wear face powder.

The required production tolerances and the meticulous care that was expended in producing a gyro that was as near to perfect as possible are evidence of the criticality of the component. The quality of the guidance system and, ultimately, the effectiveness of Thor as a weapon system were largely dependent upon the gyros performing to their specification; only when the missile achieved the true ballistic trajectory was the task of the gyros and the systems of which they were a part complete. Necessarily, the description of the flight control sub-systems that were responsible for the control and navigation of the missile's flight will make many references to the work of these gyros. It may be appropriate, therefore, to take a look inside the seemingly mysterious world of the gyro.

Gyroscopes

Gyro-dynamics is a complex, yet very interesting subject, steeped in mathematics. Fortunately, it is only really necessary to have an appreciation of the two basic properties of the gyroscope in order to follow the description of the inner workings of Thor's guidance and control system. The following text describes these properties and then moves on to examine the behaviour of a gyro when forces are applied. Various types of gyro and their application are discussed.

The diagrams that appear in this section are reproduced by kind permission of the commandant, Central Flying School, Royal Air Force College, Cranwell.

Gyroscopes were not a new invention. They had been in use as spinning self-balancing toys in many different civilisations, including Classical Greece. All these devices, however, employed the same principle of conservation of angular momentum.

Gyroscope was the name given to the device we recognise today by a French physicist, Jean Bernard Léon Foucault (1819–1868), in 1852. Foucalt used a very large rotating sphere, invented by a German, Johann Bohnenberger, as a way of demonstrating the Earth's rotation and named it accordingly from the Greek *gyros* (circle or rotation) and *skopeein* (to see).

It is interesting to note that the behaviour of a conventional gyroscope (one which possesses a spinning wheel or rotor) is governed by a set of physical laws that are identical to those that apply to the Earth itself. There are two basic properties to consider with regards to the gyro. These are the properties of rigidity in inertial space and precession.

Inertial space can be considered as a part of space, away from the earth, assumed to have fixed coordinates so that the trajectory of an object, such as a missile, may be calculated in relation to it.

Possibly the most obvious part of a simple gyroscope when its casing is removed is the gyro wheel, or rotor. The rotor spins rapidly around its axis (the axle supporting it) and is generally mounted in a frame or a series of frames, known as gimbals. The gimbals are pivoted within an outer frame (which is usually attached to the vehicle structure) and vary in number so as to achieve the degrees of freedom required, depending upon the intended application.

The first property, rigidity, is, put very simply, the inertia of the rotor. It occurs when the rotor is made to spin. Once the rotor is spinning at a constant angular velocity, and therefore constant angular momentum (which is the product of its mass 'x' its velocity), the rotor tends to remain in its plane of rotation, unless an external force (a torque) is applied to it—simply, until such an external torque is applied, the gyro's spin axis will continue to be aligned to the same point in inertial space that it was originally set to. This property is defined in the first law of gyro-dynamics. The gyro will resist any attempt to alter its position, the magnitude of the rigidity being proportional to the speed of rotation, the mass of the rotor and also the effective radius of the rotor. Therefore, the greater the rigidity, the greater the disturbing force needs to be in order to influence the gyro. The rotor is generally constructed with its mass concentrated towards the outer rim.

The second property of the gyro, precession, may be a little more obscure than the property of rigidity. Basically, if an external force, large enough to deflect the gyroscope spin axis, is applied to the gyroscope, the force does not act in the direction it is applied. It actually acts at a point 90 degrees from the point of application, measured in the direction of rotation of the rotor. The following diagram may help to illustrate the phenomena.

With reference to the diagram, the gyroscope is spinning around its axis, marked X-X1. A mass, denoted as 'M', is now placed on the inner of the two gimbal rings. It can clearly be seen that the mass will produce a downward force, 'F', thereby producing a torque, 'T', about the Y-Y1 axis.

The immediate effect of the mass being placed on the gimbal ring is that the gyro spin axis will tilt through a small angle, in the diagram, after which, perhaps surprisingly, there is no further movement about the Y-Y1 axis. The actual value of the angle is so small that it does not warrant further consideration.

The gyro spin axis will now start to turn at a constant angular velocity around the axis that is perpendicular to the axes X-X1 and Y-Y1—that is, the Z-Z1 axis—this motion being known as precession. The property of precession is defined in the second law of gyro-dynamics.

The diagram below may be useful in summing up the foregoing text.

Assume that the torque applied is a force at right angles to the plane of spin and is applied at a point on the rim of the rotor. Proceed around the rim of the rotor

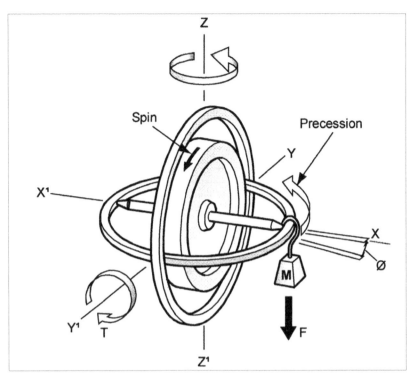

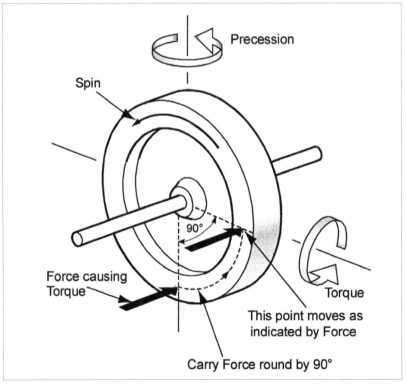

in the direction of spin through an angle of 90 degrees. The applied torque will appear to act at this point, causing the rotor to precess as shown.

The gyro is generally described as having three axes:

The input axis: the axis about which the force that causes the gyro to precess is applied.

The output axis: the axis about which the gyro will precess and on which the precession will be measured by the pick-offs.

The spin axis: the axis about which the gyro rotor rotates.

Gyroscopes are classified in the terms of the quantity they measure:

Rate gyro: this gyro will measure the rate of angular displacement of a vehicle.

Rate integrating gyro: this gyro will measure the integral of an input with respect to time.

Displacement gyro: this gyro will measure the angular displacement from a known datum.

Thor employed displacement gyros and rate gyros in the auto pilot sub-system, with rate integrating gyros and pendulous integrating gyro accelerometers (which will be described separately) utilised in the inertial guidance system.

The rate gyro diagram below shows a gyro having freedom about only one axis, the axis Y-Y1.

Should the frame attached to the gyro be turned about its vertical axis (Z-Z1), which is perpendicular to both the axes X-X1 and Y-Y1, the spin axis will precess around the Y-Y1 axis. This precession would continue until the direction of rotor spin coincides with the direction of the applied turning force around the axis Z-Z1.

Let it now be assumed that the freedom of this gyro about the axis Y-Y1 is restrained in some way—for example, by springs attached between the gimbal and the frame, as in the diagram below.

Should the gyro now be turned around the axis Z-Z1, the precession about the Y-Y1 axis is opposed by the torque generated by the springs. Any torque that opposes precession causes a secondary precession that acts in the same direction as the original torque. Assuming that the rate at which the frame is being turned remains constant, the precession around the Y-Y1 axis will continue, with one spring being stretched while the other is being compressed, causing an increase in spring torque. There will be a point at which the spring torque will produce secondary precession around the axis Z-Z1 equal to and in the same direction as the original turning force.

At this point, the turning rate and the precession rate of the gyro will be equal and no further torque will be applied by the turning. It should be clear that a certain turning force will be balanced by a certain spring force, and so, naturally, any change in the rate of the turning force around the Z-Z1 axis would require

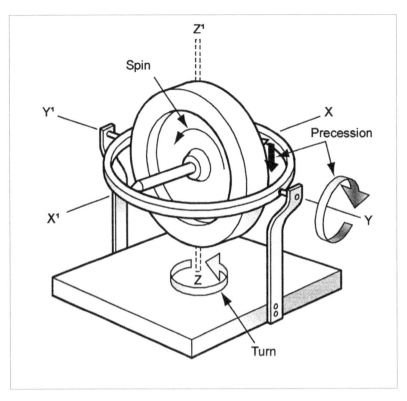

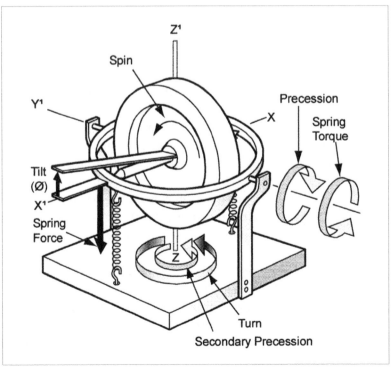

a different spring force to produce the equilibrium described. It will be seen, therefore, that the angle in the diagram above, which is the deflection of the gyro's spin axis, is a measure of the rate of the turning force. It should be noted that the above diagrams are for illustrative purposes only and do not represent the actual configuration of the gyros in Thor.

A major issue with the development of gyros of the accuracy required for inertial navigation systems was that of gyro drift caused by the friction developed in the gimbal bearings.

There had been much research conducted with a view to reducing gimbal friction. One technique was to use an air or gas bearing, where the gyro is supported by a layer of air between the gimbal and its case. This type had its roots back in the final stages of the Second World War and had been in development for the German V2 missile. At the end of the war, a great many German scientists had been transferred to the United States and this work continued at the Redstone Arsenal of the US Army, Huntsville, Alabama. The scientists there succeeded in developing a high-performance air bearing gyro and these were employed in the missile that was originally Thor's competitor, Jupiter, built by the Chrysler Corporation.

Another solution to the issue of gimbal friction had been developed by MIT. The gyros were liquid-floated integrating gyros. In these gyros, the gimbal and rotor assemblies of the gyroscope were floated in a dense fluid, in a practice known as viscous damping. This technique achieved a condition of neutral buoyancy that was unaffected by any accelerations applied to the gyro. The gimbal axes were located on jewelled bearings, but friction was extremely low due to these bearings being unloaded. These liquid-floated rate integrating gyros were the type employed in Thor's guidance.

Liquid-floated gyros were not without their issues. The density of the viscous fluid had to be kept constant and so the temperature of the fluid needed to be carefully controlled. This was achieved by the means of a thermostat within the gyro casing. It was also a requirement that the temperature outside the gyro casing was controlled within a relatively small range in order to protect the operation of the fluid thermostat; therefore, a cooling system was required to control ambient temperature within the stabilised platform container. However, it had to be so arranged as not to produce a temperature gradient across the gyro, which, by causing convection currents within the fluid, might give rise to spurious torques being detected.

A rate-integrating gyro is one that is suspended such that it can move about only one axis apart from the axis of rotation. Its operation is similar to the basic rate gyro described above, except for the fact that the springs shown in the simple diagram are not present. The only opposition to gimbal rotation around the output axis was the viscosity of the fluid (the fluid in Thor's gyros was a fluorocarbon, about twice as dense as water).

The main purpose of a rate-integrating gyro is to detect any turning moments around the input axis.

The rotor of the gyroscope is pivoted in an inner can (the gimbal), which is itself floated in an outer can. All the controls, pick-offs, and torquers are contained in the outer can. The heaters may be in a jacket surrounding the gyroscope.

The gyro operates by sensing any rotation about the input (sensitive) axis, which would cause the gyro inner can to precess about its output axis. The gimbal initially precesses to a turning rate such that the restraint provided by the viscous fluid equals the applied torque. The gimbal then rotates at a steady rate about the output axis proportional to the applied torque. The relative motion between the inner and outer cans is detected and measured by the pick-offs (see below). The output of which, expressed as either an angle or a voltage depending upon application, is the summation of the amount of input turn derived from the rate and duration of turn and is therefore the integral of the input turning rate.

The detection of the angular measurement about a gyroscope's sensitive axis is the function of the pick-offs, which generate electrical signals proportional to the movement. The torquers work almost in the opposite sense. Electrical signals, proportional to the required correcting torque, are sent to the torquers, which cause the gyro to precess at the required rate.

Pick-offs and torquers are generally of the induction type. They may be separate from each other or may indeed be combined into one unit. If the two elements

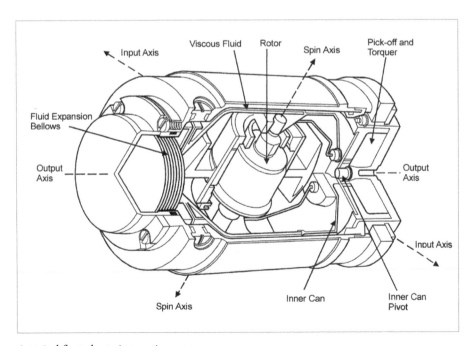

A typical floated rate-integrating gyro.

should be in a single unit, the pick-offs would be powered by AC and the torquers by DC to avoid interaction between the electric fields.

An important parameter in gyro-dynamics is gimbal gain, which is the ratio of input to output. A high ratio would allow the gyro to detect very small input rates. The factors influencing gimbal gain are the size of the gimbal, the mass of the rotor and the viscosity of the fluid in which the inner can is floated. The fluid temperature affects the viscosity of the fluid and therefore the gimbal gain. In order to achieve a constant gimbal gain and consequently consistent system performance, the fluid temperature has to be controlled within very close tolerances. This is the reason that the gyro heaters on Thor were so closely monitored, in a practice that came to be known by the launch crews as bird watching.

Errors, known as cross-coupling errors, can be introduced when rotation is sensed around an already displaced input axis. For this reason, it is essential to limit the amount of inner can precession to avoid this error.

Flight Control System
The missile had to be placed on a path in space, so that when the re-entry vehicle separated from the missile body, it continued along a ballistic trajectory to intersect the position of the target. Stabilisation and steering of the missile to achieve arrival at this point during the powered phase of flight was the function of the flight control system.

The flight control system of the missile consisted of two subsystems: the autopilot and the inertial guidance system. The autopilot controlled missile attitude during flight by issuing commands to the servo valves of the engine thrust chamber hydraulic actuators. The hydraulic actuators then moved to regulate the angular displacement of the thrust chambers, controlling the direction of the forces acting upon the missile.

The inertial guidance subsystem provided continuous corrections to the missile's flight attitude in order to select the optimum trajectory to the target.

Each Thor was pre-programmed with two possible targets. The chosen target was selected and the relevant guidance data entered into the missile on the ground.

Both elements of the flight control system worked in unison to provide control over the two phases of the missile's powered flight, which were the sustainer (main engine) phase and the vernier phase.

The first portion of the missile's flight was pre-programmed specifically for the selected target. During the first few seconds of flight, a roll voltage was applied to the autopilot subsystem and the missile rotated about its roll axis to establish the yaw axis of the missile in a vertical plane through the desired cut-off trajectory. At the end of the roll manoeuvre, the belly of the missile was facing the target.

A programmed missile pitch-over sequence was then initiated. This achieved two objectives. It resulted in the missile leaving the initial vertical climb and flying down range towards the required position in space and, very importantly, steered

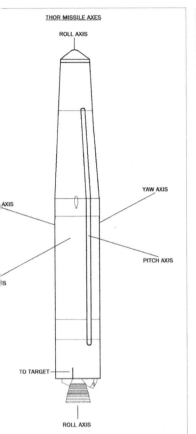

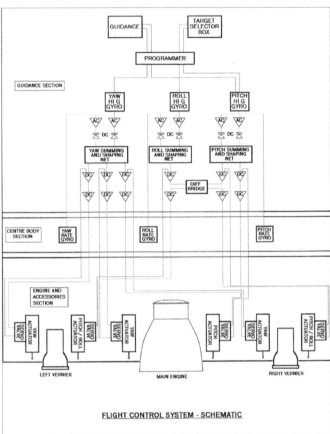

the missile through the atmosphere such that a 'gravity turn' was approximated. A gravity turn results when the missile angle of attack (the angle between the reference line of the missile, in this case the roll axis, and the airflow relative to the missile) and consequently the aerodynamic forces normal to the rol axis are at zero. This pre-programmed pitch profile is alternatively referred to as a 'zero lift' or a 'zero angle of attack' pitch programme. It was utilised to prevent structural failure in the missile as a result of aerodynamic forces. The aerodynamic forces involved are lift and drag. The drag force is directed along the roll axis while the lift force acts at the normal to the missile axis, the point at which the resultant aerodynamic force vectors act on the missile being known as the centre of pressure (CP). The axial strength of the missile is much greater than the transverse strength and so the forces normal to the roll axis (i.e. lift) must be minimised for flight through the atmosphere, otherwise the aerodynamic lift forces would produce bending moments along the missile axis that could break the long, slender missile. Maintaining a zero angle of attack ensured that the missile did not develop the potentially damaging lift forces. The commanded missile attitude turning rates required for the approximation of the gravity turn were obtained from a simulation based on a complex equation that involved, among other factors, the missile inertial velocity, the Earth's angular velocity, and the wind velocity. In practicality, the wind velocity was usually neglected in the calculations. Having obtained the required turning rates, these were then set out in the format required for use by the missile programmer. The point at which the aerodynamic forces (q) are greatest (max-q) was passed while the missile was executing the pre-programmed pitch sequence.

On completion of the pre-programmed phase of flight, the inertial guidance system would take over the navigation of the missile based on the data entered into the missile for the specific target. The guidance would calculate the optimum flight path to reach the required point in space, and away from the atmosphere, the steering commands produced would not subject the missile to the dangers of aerodynamic loading.

The autopilot subsystem consisted of a programmer, gyroscopes, filter servo-amplifiers, and associated circuitry. The programmer contained switching circuits, which generated signals to control the programmed functions of the missile's flight. This package was referred to as the control and electronics assembly (CEA). The flight control system also controlled the sequencing of other major in-flight operations, sustainer engine cut-off, vernier engine cut-off, re-entry vehicle separation, and the firing of the retro rockets.

The autopilot subsystem utilised a total of six gyroscopes, three displacement gyroscopes and three rate gyroscopes. The displacement gyroscopes were mounted in the guidance section in the nose of the missile, while the rate gyroscopes were housed in the short centre body section of the airframe between the fuel and oxidiser tanks.

The displacement gyroscopes (which were two-degrees-of-freedom gyroscopes) provided a datum about which angular displacement could be measured, enabling their use for attitude correction or steering commands as required. Before launch, the displacement gyroscopes were set to a 'zero error' position and this provided the missile with a 'zero reference' position for flight. Each displacement gyroscope was mounted so as to sense deviations, in terms of angle and direction, in its particular reference plane (pitch, yaw, or roll). If the missile deviated from the desired course, the affected gyroscope would precess, causing the gimbals to rotate and consequently change the position of an associated signal generator armature; this then generated an error signal proportional to the amount of missile angular displacement from the yaw, roll, and pitch reference planes.

The rate gyroscopes, which were in fixed reference planes, sensed the rate of missile attitude changes and provided signals proportional to the rate (angular velocity) of displacement from the yaw, pitch, and roll reference planes.

Output from the gyroscopes, in the form of error voltages, was fed to the filter-servo-amplifier packages.

The filter-servo-amplifier packages contained the circuitry required to convert gyroscope error signals into input data for the servo-amplifiers. The servo-amplifiers operated the servo-valves of the engine actuators, enabling the hydraulic system to change the position of the engines thrust chambers and thus counteract the deviations sensed by the gyroscopes, correcting the missile's attitude.

Signals were routed through three summing and shaping networks, one for each of the three control axes—pitch, roll, and yaw. The summing amplifier was used for combining multiple inputs, in this case from the displacement and the rate gyroscopes, while the shaping circuit adapted system response to suit the characteristics and flight path of the missile.

The yaw summing and shaping net routed signals to the yaw actuators of the main thrust chamber and of both vernier engines. A yaw command would cause all three of the thrust chambers to move in the same appropriate direction.

The pitch summing and shaping net routed signals to the pitch actuator of the main engine thrust chamber and via a differential bridge to the pitch and roll actuators of both vernier engines. A pitch command would cause all three of the thrust chambers to move in the same appropriate direction.

The roll summing and shaping net routed signals via a differential bridge to the pitch and roll actuators of the two vernier engines only. A roll command would cause the vernier engine thrust chambers to move in opposite directions to induce a roll in the appropriate direction.

It will have been noted that although the two vernier engines had dedicated yaw actuators, roll and pitch functions were provided by the same actuator; the appropriate flight control function being signalled by the differential bridge, which would also have allowed differential movement (mixing) of the thrust chambers to provide simultaneous roll and pitch functions.

Feedback transducers on the actuators sent back signals to the filter-amplifier package that were proportional to engine thrust chamber displacement. Such a feedback signal opposed the gyroscope output signal and caused the engine to return to the null position during an attitude correction sequence.

When not in operation, the actuators formed a rigid link, keeping the thrust chambers in the required position.

At the moment of launch, three major events took place in the missile flight control system. The programmer started to run, the inertial navigation stabilised platform became space referenced, and the Vg clutches engaged, this last action allowing the potentiometers to drive.

The programmer, as it started, ran an autopilot trace, a coded tape that was read by the programmer. Due to the configuration of the coding on the tape, instructions were passed to the flight control system to fly the first portion of the mission profile, directing the missile toward the selected target. This control method is very similar to the paper roll that can be fed through a pianola or player piano device to play music.

For the first two seconds after launch, the missile was in free flight. Over the next eight seconds, the programmer would command the missile roll manoeuvre.

This phase always took eight seconds, irrespective of the number of degrees that the missile needed to roll through and therefore the rate of roll was scheduled accordingly. Including this manoeuvre in the flight profile allowed a certain degree of freedom for the target planners, providing an arc that would include a choice of potential targets. The geographical coverage provided by this arc would be chosen at the time of launch site planning, by selection of the orientation of the launch pad centreline. Once built, this pad orientation was quite literally set in stone. The missile could be rolled a maximum of 15 degrees in either direction away from the orientation of the centreline of the launch pad, this limit being largely due to physical constraints in the azimuth alignment of the stabilised platform for the inertial guidance system. The roll manoeuvre, at the end of which the belly of the missile was facing the target, established the yaw axis of the missile in a vertical plane through the desired cut off trajectory. The roll was achieved by the application of a roll voltage to the autopilot subsystem, which in turn signalled the vernier engines to roll the missile. With the roll manoeuvre completed, the remainder of the pre-programmed flight profile was achieved by means of the pitch programme. The programmer did not provide steering commands in the yaw axis.

The programmer commanded the required missile attitude through the medium of the displacement gyroscopes. The displacement gyroscope reference planes were controlled by torque signal amplifiers and could be altered for steering purposes. To change the missile flight path, the programmer would send a torque signal to the torque generator of the appropriate displacement gyroscope (pitch or roll). The torque generator applied a torque force, which rotated the gyroscope gimbal and consequently changed the gyroscope's spin axis position in relation to its previous position. The displacement gyroscope was simply set to provide a new datum. The rotation of the gimbal caused its signal generator to produce an error signal. In turn, this caused the missile to change attitude until the airframe control axis (pitch or roll) corresponded to the new gyroscope reference, about which angular displacement and direction could again be measured in order to correct any deviation to the new flight path.

The pitch programme was completed by, typically, t+108 seconds—that is, 108 seconds after lift-off. The pre-programmed portion of the flight was now complete and the missile had arrived at an approximate position. From this point, the inertial guidance system would take over and issue steering commands, again through the displacement gyroscopes, to control the missile along one of a number of alternate flight paths for final positioning in space.

The guidance and control group controls weighed 737 lb (334 kg).

Inertial Guidance System

The basic principle of inertial navigation is to measure the individual components of a vehicle's acceleration with respect to a known set of axes.

Subject to the initial conditions being known, the measured accelerations can be integrated with respect to time to produce the component velocities. Should the distance travelled along each of the axes be required, it can be obtained by means of a second round of integration, this time of the velocity components.

Therefore, the starting point for inertial navigation is the acceleration information because it is the only kinematic quantity (concerned with the motion without reference to force or mass) that can be measured within the subject vehicle itself. Acceleration information is derived through Newton's laws of dynamics, utilising a device known as an accelerometer.

The purpose of an accelerometer is to measure any acceleration of the body in which it is placed. In its simplest form, it could be visualised as a mass held between two springs, contained so that it can only move along the line of the springs. Acceleration could be measured by the action of an indicator, attached to the mass, moving against a fixed scale.

If this accelerometer were to be placed in a vehicle with the springs aligned along, for example, its longitudinal axis, any acceleration of the vehicle in this plane would cause the inertia of the mass to compress one spring, while causing the other to elongate. The indicator attached to the mass would then provide an indication against the scale. If the acceleration is steady, the indicator will remain at the same deflection. Should the vehicle settle at a steady speed, however, the mass and therefore its indicator will return to the zero position; this steady speed must be remembered during any speed (and distance) calculations that may be required. If the vehicle were to decelerate, the mass would move in the opposite direction by an amount proportional to the rate of deceleration. An everyday example of this principle, with which we are all familiar, is the feeling of being pressed back into the seat as a vehicle accelerates and tending to lean forward again as the vehicle decelerates or brakes.

A second accelerometer could be placed along the lateral line of the vehicle to indicate any acceleration in this plane and a third could be employed for the measurement of acceleration in the vertical plane. This arrangement would then be suitable for a vehicle, such as a missile, that has 6 degrees of freedom—that is, moves in three dimensions.

This is exactly how the accelerometers in Thor were arranged. The axes of the three accelerometers were mutually perpendicular and defined the X, Y, and Z axes of a reference coordinate system, also known as a reference frame, in order for accelerations to be measured along each particular plane.

The reference coordinate system was established and maintained as part of the launch countdown sequence during guidance alignment. The X axis accelerometer was aligned to the target azimuth. This automatically orientated the Y and Z axes accelerometers to sense lateral and vertical accelerations respectively, while the X axis accelerometer orientation would result in the sensing of accelerations down range (i.e., towards the target).

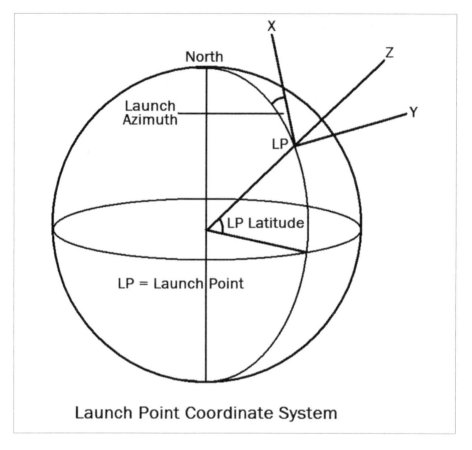

Launch Point Coordinate System

The accelerometers measured the accelerations to which the missile was subject, usually expressed in terms of feet per second per second. If the acceleration is known, then the velocity can be calculated:

Velocity = Acceleration × Time.

A very simple example to illustrate this would be to assume that a body experiences a steady acceleration of 50 feet per second per second for a period of ten seconds:

At the end of one second, the velocity is 50 feet/second.
At the end of two seconds, the velocity is 100 feet/second.
At the end of three seconds, the velocity is 150 feet/second.
Continue this for ten seconds, after which the velocity would be 500 feet/second.

This simple example employs a steady acceleration and in reality this will not be the case. Thor began its flight at zero velocity and, with its engines at full power for the duration of their burn, the missile would accelerate up to the moment of vernier engine cut off. Therefore, a much more accurate method of calculating the missile velocity at any given instant (the key to solving Thor's guidance formula) was required. For this, the system's designers turned to the mathematical process of integral calculus. Thor's accelerometers, rather than being a contained spring as in the simple explanation above, were in reality Pendulous Integrating Gyroscopic Accelerometers (PIGA); there was one for each of the three reference planes.

A PIGA possesses a high level of accuracy and has the advantage of also being able to perform the process of integration required to convert the accelerations of the missile into a velocity.

The gyro is provided with a known unbalance (in the form of a pendulous mass) about its output gimbal axis. Any acceleration acting parallel to the input axis will therefore produce a torque proportional to that acceleration about the gyro output axis. The gyro will move a small angle around the output axis and produce a signal from the output pick-off; when amplified, this will cause the servo motor to rotate the gyro about its input axis at a rate such that the precession torque created balances precisely the unbalance torque caused by the acceleration. In doing this, the pick-off returns to its near null position. The rate of rotation about the input axis is therefore proportional to the acceleration, so that the input angle will be proportional to the time integral of the acceleration—that is, the velocity.

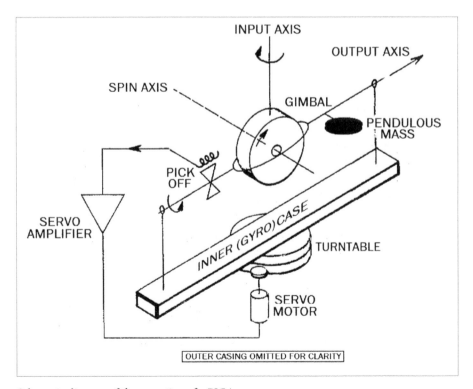

Schematic diagram of the operation of a PIGA.

The PIGA was based on an accelerometer developed for the German V2 ballistic missile by Dr Fritz Mueller (one of the scientists brought back to Huntsville, Alabama at the end of the war) and was known among the German rocket scientists as the MMIA (the Mueller Mechanical Integrating Accelerometer).

An MMIA accelerometer, recovered from an unexploded V2, had been presented to Dr Charles Stark Draper of MIT's instrumentation laboratory. Dr Draper combined the principles of his liquid-floated integrating gyroscopes with the recovered V2 accelerometer by floating the pendulum-gyroscope portion in a viscous fluid. He suggested the generic title of PIGA for the device due to the addition of various refinements, such as electromagnetic or optical sensing of pendulum position, which were later employed on the Titan II, Polaris, and Minuteman missile systems.

Clearly, for accelerations to be sensed correctly in their respective planes, it is absolutely vital that the accelerometers remain strictly aligned to their reference planes. This was achieved by mounting the accelerometers on a stabilised platform and ensuring that the platform maintained its position relative to the reference coordinate system, irrespective of the attitude of the missile itself.

The stabilised platform (the heart of the guidance system) was suspended in a system of gimbals, three in the AC Achiever fitted to Thor. The gimbals were mounted within a fixed frame attached to the missile airframe, with their axes mutually at right angles—each was provided with a servo motor. The gimbal system ensured that the stabilised platform and, therefore, the accelerometers were isolated from missile manoeuvring. To counter any tendency for the platform to move with the missile during a manoeuvre, the platform carried three single-degree-of-freedom gyroscopes, which were set with their input axes mutually at right angles and aligned before launch so that their null positions corresponded with the axes of the reference frame. The gyros spin axis was fixed with reference to inertial space and any movement of the platform away from its stabilised position would be detected by one or more of the gyroscopes; the associated error pick-offs would cause error signals, proportional to the change in platform attitude, to be generated and sent to the gimbal servo motors that would drive the gimbals to achieve correct alignment on the platform. Once back in the correct orientation, the error signals would cease and the servo-motor would stop driving the gimbals.

Electrical resolvers, placed within the gimbal system, sensed any relative motion between the missile airframe and the stabilised platform. The signals generated provided an attitude reference for the missile and were used in pitch, roll, and yaw control.

In summary, the key elements of an inertial guidance system are the stabilised platform and the accelerometers. The purpose of the stabilised platform is to maintain the accelerometers in alignment with their respective reference planes, allowing accurate measurement of the accelerations to which the vehicle is subject.

The output from the accelerometers, in the form of a voltage proportional to the velocities sensed (the key to solving Thor's guidance formula), provides the information

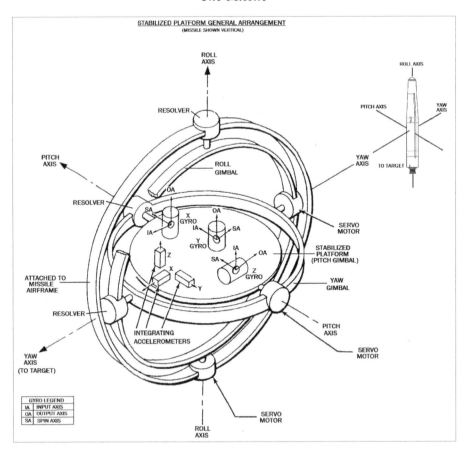

required by the guidance system computer for the completion of the second, guided portion of the powered flight profile—that is, the final positioning in space.

The Guidance Solution

Thor's on board analogue computer provided the guidance solution, guiding the missile during flight along a path in space so that at the completion of the powered flight phase, the re-entry vehicle will follow a freefall trajectory to its predetermined target.

Ballistic trajectories, using an example artillery shell, were discussed earlier. There is a very important concept of which to be aware, and in order to provide an explanation, it is to the example shell that we shall, briefly, return. A shell fired from a gun will achieve its maximum velocity at the moment of its leaving the muzzle and it will follow a true ballistic flight path to its target. Looking at this a little more deeply, this would mean that, at any given instant during its flight, the velocity of the shell will be equal to the correlated velocity, which can be defined as the velocity that the shell (or missile) must possess in order to reach the target in the flight time remaining. This is a very important point to grasp and will be referred to frequently later in the text.

So far, only the true ballistic flight path has been considered and this is the flight path that the re-entry vehicle will need to follow in order to reach the intended target. The point in space at which the re-entry vehicle separates from the missile airframe is analogous to the point at which the shell described earlier leaves the muzzle of the gun. The re-entry vehicle is at its correlated velocity (Vc) and will therefore reach the intended target in the flight time remaining.

Positioning of the missile to this point in space is achieved in the phase of flight, during which the missile follows a powered ballistic flight path, initially on a pre-programmed trajectory, with the final positioning achieved under the influence of the guidance system.

During the 1950s, two scientists at MIT's Instrumentation Laboratory, Dr J. Halcombe 'Hal' Laning (Deputy Associate Director of the Instrumentation Laboratory 1955–1980) and Richard H. Battin (Adjunct Professor, Department of Aeronautics and Astronautics, MIT, 1951), devised an alternative to the existing methods of missile guidance. The technique used a simplified computational geometry, most of the calculations for which could be performed on the ground. This was particularly suited to missiles that had a trajectory that consisted of a relatively short powered flight followed by a ballistic phase during which the missile's payload would coast to its target under the influence of gravity. Thor was an ideal candidate for this type of guidance solution. The new technique was named Q-Guidance. 'Q' is a constant that represents many variable factors affecting a missile's flight. It is used to convert the distance of the missile from the equivalent point on an ideal trajectory into the appropriate change of correlated velocity. The objective of the system used in Thor was to hit a specific target after a specified time of flight, in this case fifteen minutes. Later Q-Guidance systems, such as that employed for Polaris, did not have fixed time of flight schemes. The major difference from the established methods of guidance and a missile with Q-Guidance was that the latter had no need to return to a pre-computed flight path should it deviate for some reason, and it had no need to be specifically aware of its current position. The missile with Q-Guidance did, however, know where it needed to get to. It would instead calculate a new optimum flight path from where it was to a point where the payload could be released, and it would reach the target in the flight time remaining.

An advantage of having a fixed time of flight scheme was that it simplified the missile's on-board equipment and reduced the demand for in flight computing capability. By knowing the flight time, certain allowances could now be made before flight for factors that would otherwise be variable.

Two of the issues that this addressed were raised by the characteristics of our planet itself, which were discussed briefly during the earlier part of this chapter and which will now be examined in a little more detail.

If the Earth was not rotating, the aiming point for the missile would always coincide with the target location at the time of launch, regardless of the duration of the missile's flight. The Earth, however, is rotating and therefore the missile must be aimed at the point that will be occupied by the target at the moment the missile strikes. Clearly, the longer the flight time of the missile, the greater the distance eastward the target will traverse; however, the distance that the target will travel during the flight time of the missile is actually very simple to calculate. Although the rate of the Earth's rotation remains constant at, for illustrative purposes, 15 degrees per hour, (360 (degrees) divided by twenty-four (hours)), the speed of rotation of a point on the surface varies as a function of the cosine of its latitude. For example, a point on the equator will have a rotational speed of 15 × 60 (calculated by the number of degrees (per hour) multiplied by the number of minutes of arc in a degree) = 900 minutes of arc per hour. As one minute of arc at the equator is taken to be equivalent to 1 nautical mile, then the rotational speed of a point on the equator will be 900 nautical miles per hour, or knots. The rotational speed of a point away from the equator will be equivalent to 900 (the rotational speed at the equator) multiplied by the cosine of its latitude; therefore, for a point situated at 60 degrees' latitude, its rotational speed will be 900 × 0.5 (the cosine of angle 60 degrees) = 450 knots. For a target at latitude 60 degrees, the target would travel 112.5 nautical miles for the fifteen-minute flight time of the missile.

The Earth, as we know, is not a perfect sphere; it is an oblate spheroid, having a bulge in the middle regions and is slightly flattened at the poles, being more of a tangerine shape. Errors in navigation due to this factor alone would be in the order of some 3 miles per 1,500 miles (Thor's operational range) if this feature of the planet were not accounted for.

To sum up the foregoing and to introduce some new terms, the target position is the position of the target at the time the missile is launched. The target's predicted position is the position (at the time of launch) that the target will be at the moment of impact. The distance between the target position and the target's predicted position is due to the rate of the Earth's rotation at the target's latitude, as illustrated in the example calculation above.

The aim point is the point at which the missile must be aimed so that it will hit the target, allowing for the Earth's rotation during the time of flight. The distance between the aim point and the target's predicted position is due to the rate of the Earth's rotation at the launch point. If the target and launch point are on the same latitude, this is not an issue as the launch would be either due east or due west, but coincidences like this rarely occur in reality. If the target and the launch point are at different latitudes, the eastward velocity of the launch point results in an effective change to the firing azimuth and this has to be allowed for. This is relatively easily calculated for a fixed flight time of the missile.

It should also be appreciated that the term velocity is a vector quantity and therefore has both magnitude and direction. When the term velocity is used, both of these properties are implied.

As noted earlier, at the moment of the missile's lift-off, the velocity is virtually zero; therefore, the velocity required to ensure that the re-entry vehicle reaches the target in the flight time remaining is large. After lift-off, the velocity of the missile

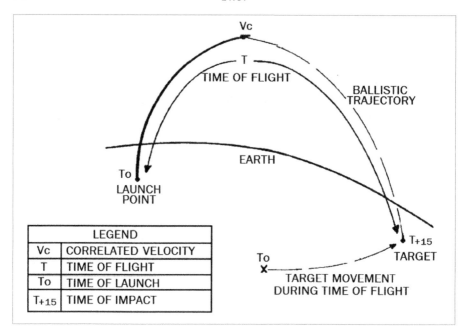

LEGEND	
Vc	CORRELATED VELOCITY
T	TIME OF FLIGHT
To	TIME OF LAUNCH
T+15	TIME OF IMPACT

increases only relatively slowly due to aerodynamic and gravitational effects, and so, initially, this stage of the flight will account for only a small percentage of the total distance to be travelled to the target. An important concept to be aware of here is that of the velocity to be gained (Vg). The powered missile always has some actual velocity, the velocity of the missile (Vm). There is also the correlated velocity (Vc) that the missile must possess in order to reach the target in the time remaining. The difference between the actual velocity of the missile and the correlated velocity must therefore be the velocity to be gained (Vg). This can be expressed as $Vg = Vc - Vm$. The velocity to be gained is continuously reducing during powered flight, and at the end of the powered flight phase, it will be at zero. At this point, the missile will be at the correlated velocity; it will then continue in free fall along the ballistic trajectory to its target.

The missile's inertial guidance system and computer measured the actual velocity and determined the correlated velocity for every instant, comparing the two. When the two values were equal, the engine power was cut. The computer also calculated the velocity to be gained for every point along the powered flight path. The calculations were based on the flight time remaining and measurements were taken by the accelerometers, using a differential equation where a 'Q' matrix (hence the name of the technique) is defined by a symmetric three-by-three time-varying matrix. The calculation of this matrix was performed on the ground at the target planning stage, and experience demonstrated that the matrix was only slowly time varying, so very few values of 'Q' (the solution of the calculations) corresponding to different times during the flight needed to be stored on board the missile, which further simplified the work of Thor's analogue guidance computer.

A relatively simple guidance strategy was to apply acceleration—that is, engine thrust—in the direction of the velocity to be gained (Vg). This had the effect of making the actual velocity come closer to Vc. One way to bring the thrust vector into alignment with the Vg was to steer at a rate proportional to the cross product between Vc and Vg. This was used to set the autopilot steering rate and became known as cross-product steering, which could be achieved quite easily in the guidance computer. When all components of Vg were small, the main engine power was cut, leaving the vernier engines to provide the final, delicate adjustments to the trajectory to bring the components of Vg to zero. At this point, the verniers too were cut. The missile was now on a true ballistic trajectory.

To sum up, the purpose of the missile is to reach that one velocity (Vc) that will permit free fall to the target in the flight time remaining. It was the function of the guidance system to steer the missile so that it would reach this velocity and to determine when it had done so. The guidance system accomplished this by having the computer continuously calculating the missile's velocity and the flight time remaining. At some instance during flight, it would be determined that the missile's velocity and the correlated velocity were equal. At that time, the engines were cut out and the missile would free fall towards the target along the ballistic trajectory.

Finally, before moving on to look at the operation of the guidance and control system, it may be helpful to review some important points that have appeared in the text.

Correlated velocity: the velocity that a body must possess in order to reach the target in the flight time remaining. A body following a ballistic trajectory travels at every instant at the correlated velocity. This velocity is always changing, but its value is always correlated. In order to put a missile into a ballistic trajectory, it is only necessary to impart to it at some instant the correlated velocity. If the power is then removed, the missile will continue along the correct ballistic flight path, always possessing correlated velocity.

Velocity to be gained: the difference between the actual velocity of the missile and the correlated velocity.

Target position: the position of the target at the time of launch.

Target predicted position: the position on the Earth's surface at the time of launch, which the target will occupy at the moment of impact.

Aim (or aiming) point: the point on the Earth's surface at which the missile is aimed, in order that the missile will hit the target, allowing for the rotation of the Earth during the time of flight.

Each Thor was equipped with two pre-determined targets. The required target, simply entitled 'target one' or 'target two', was chosen on the ground at the ground support equipment. The guidance and control system incorporated a target selector box and a programmer, part of the CEA, which contained the autopilot traces for both targets. It also selected and flew the roll and pitch programme for the first, pre-programmed phase of the powered flight.

Should a Thor be subsequently allocated a different target, the roll and pitch programme would require updating to reflect its new destination and this was a task for the technicians at the complex's main base. A 107 Squadron Thor at Tuddenham required such a change, this being recorded in the squadron's ORB, which stated simply that there had been a target change ordered that necessitated a change of settings in the CEA, which was returned to the RIM.

The pre-programmed phase saw the missile rise on launch in free flight for the first two seconds and then, over the following eight seconds, complete the roll manoeuvre to establish the missile's yaw axis in a vertical plane through the desired cut-off trajectory. The belly of the missile would then be directly in line with the point on the Earth's surface at which the missile was aimed. The remainder of this phase was a four-stage pitch over sequence, which occupied the period from t+10 to t+108 seconds. This approximated a gravity turn as discussed earlier in this chapter, making progress toward the required point in space and guiding Thor safely through the period where potentially destructive aerodynamic forces were at their greatest. The first pitch manoeuvre occurred in the period from t+10 to t+30, the second between t+30 and t+60, the third t+60 and t+80, and the final pitch taking place between t+80 and t+100. The programmer flew the required profile through the use of the autopilot subsystem and had access to the pitch and roll functions only.

Although the inertial guidance system (IGS) tracked the missile's progress from the moment of lift off, until the pre-programmed portion of the flight profile had been completed, it could not influence the flight path. On completion of this unguided element of the flight, the IGS took over the responsibility for the second phase, the final positioning of the missile in space.

This guided phase of the powered trajectory itself consisted of two parts. The first being that to main engine cut-off (MECO) and the second from MECO to vernier engine cut-off (VECO).

Alignment of the guidance system stabilised platform had been completed during the launch countdown, so that its X axis was aligned to the required target azimuth—the point at which the missile was aimed. At the moment of launch, the stabilised platform became space referenced—that is, it would now remain aligned with the point in inertial space to which it had been set. After lift-off, the missile, in rolling to establish its yaw axis in a vertical plane through the cut-off trajectory, brought the axes of the missile and the stabilised platform into alignment.

As the missile climbed away from the its launch pad, the accelerometers mounted on the stabilised platform measured the acceleration forces to which the missile was subject in each of three reference planes: the X axis, down-range towards the target; the Y axis, lateral accelerations; and the Z axis, measuring accelerations in the vertical plane. As they also performed the process of integration, measuring the accelerations with respect to time, the resultant accelerometer output was the missile's velocity in each plane. The major feature of Q-guidance was that the missile did not require explicit information about its position, which meant that only the one stage of integration was sufficient for navigational purposes. Positional information requires the further integration of the velocities themselves. Thor's guidance solution required the missile to acquire a certain velocity vector, at which the engines would be cut-off, the missile then following the ballistic trajectory to the target. This velocity vector was the resultant of the three component velocities measured by the accelerometers.

The solution to the guidance formula was for the computer to compare the velocities measured by the accelerometers against computed reference values, the difference being seen as velocity errors. The computer used the velocity errors to calculate commands for the autopilot subsystem to vector the engine thrust and so steer the missile in order to drive the velocity errors towards zero. When all velocity errors reached zero, the missile would be exactly on the required trajectory at the correlated velocity. In this way, despite the lack of explicit positional information, the guidance system could calculate the optimum flight path.

The initial velocity errors, which in actuality represented the Vg, were loaded into the guidance system on the ground and were, as in the case of the pitch and roll programme and the azimuth alignment of the stabilised platform, unique to the chosen target. The signals could be sent to the guidance set from the guidance control panel in the launch control trailer (LCT) or the velocity control in the electrical equipment trailer (EET). The adjust/lock switch for each channel would be set to energise the clutches of the Vg potentiometers in the airborne guidance set, allowing the operation of the counters for the X, Y, and Z channels on the ground equipment. When the counters were operated, transmitter synchros (a system whereby a generator (transmitter) and a motor (receiver) are connected by wiring, such that angular rotation or position in the transmitter is reproduced simultaneously in the receiver) sent signals to the receiver synchros for the corresponding channels in the airborne guidance set. This positioned the Vg potentiometer shafts to a specific point away from their zero reference position. The signals were sent in the form of three groups of five numbers, one group for each of the X, Y, and Z channels.

Upon launch, the Vg potentiometer clutches engaged, which allowed the potentiometers to drive. The potentiometers were driven as a result of the velocity measured in each plane, their shafts rotating accordingly, the output being a voltage that was compared to a voltage referenced to the velocity to be gained. As the missile accelerated on its flight path, the potentiometer shafts turned, the output voltage changing correspondingly, reducing the error signal voltage towards the zero reference (note: this would not be zero volts. Instead, it would be a voltage that represented a zero reference point).

On completion of the pre-programmed portion of the powered flight profile, the missile was almost certain to be away from the required trajectory. This could be for any number of reasons, but two very practical candidates would be the effects of wind (especially as the missile penetrated the high-level, high-speed jet streams that would cause the missile to physically drift) and small variations in the output engine thrust, which would affect the velocity.

The roll programme had positioned the yaw axis through the cut-off trajectory in the first few seconds of flight and any tendency to roll away from this datum during the remainder of the powered trajectory would be corrected by the autopilot. Thus the missile heading would remain constant throughout. The guidance would therefore need only to make corrections vertically and laterally to reach the required point in space. For this reason, the guidance system had access to only the pitch and yaw functions, the pitch function correcting any vertical or down-range displacement from the required trajectory, while the yaw function then corrected any lateral displacement. The guidance computer compared the velocity error (Vg) voltages to the reference voltages and determined the direction and magnitude of the correction required to drive the velocity errors towards zero. The engine thrust was then vectored via the autopilot subsystem to achieve the required change in trajectory. It must be remembered that while the guidance was correcting the trajectory, the missile was still accelerating under the influence of full power from all three of its engines. The guidance computer continued to measure the actual velocity of the missile and to calculate the Vc for every instant and compare the two values. It was, however, well within the capabilities of the inertial guidance system to complete any necessary corrections to the trajectory before the missile achieved Vc.

When all elements of the Vg were close to being zero, the guidance system issued a command to de-energise No. 1 main engine solenoid, which caused the closure of the main LOX valve and ignition fuel valve, and No. 2 main engine solenoid, which closed the gas generator and main fuel valves, resulting in MECO. The main fuel tank and lubrication oil tank pressurisation also ceased at this point. The missile's velocity was now about 25 feet per second (approximately 15 knots) short of Vc. The missile continued to accelerate much more slowly under the influence of just the two small vernier engines, which were now used for the final delicate adjustments to the trajectory. The warhead received a pre-arm signal from the guidance system. As all elements of Vg reached zero, the guidance system gave the command to de-energise the solenoid that controlled the vernier engine propellant valves, resulting in VECO. Although the main and vernier engines were cut-off when all elements of Vg were near to and on zero respectively, it was in fact the Vgx element that provided the cut off signals.

The missile was now travelling on the ballistic trajectory. The nose cone latch squibs were fired. The final signal was to fire the two ARL retro-rockets, retarding Thor's airframe to allow the nose cone a clean get away. The missile airframe would re-enter the Earth's atmosphere and burn up as a result of friction.

The nose cone would now continue alone and unguided to intersect the target position at t+15 minutes.

The guidance and control group guidance weighed 1,002 lb (455 kg).

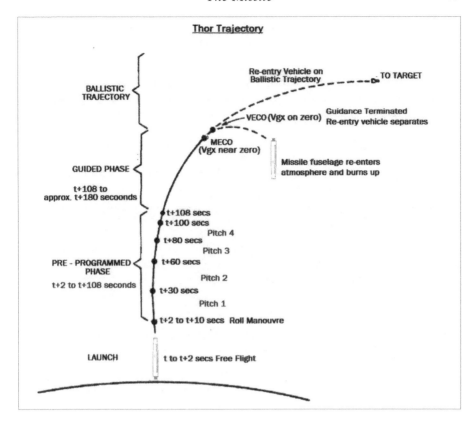

Typical Thor Mission Profile

Lift-off to t+2: the time at missile lift-off is known as 't'. During the first two seconds of flight, the missile will rise under the power of its engines with no control inputs from the flight control system

T+2 to t+10: in the next eight seconds, the missile will complete its programmed roll manoeuvre, ready to follow its flight path. This allows a target capability away from the centre line of the pad. The roll programme will always take eight seconds, the rate of roll varying with the total rolling action required.

T+10 to t+108: in this period, the missile is pitched in four stages. This portion is programmed—that is to say, it is fixed for a particular target in advance. The first pitch manoeuvre occurs in the period from t+10 to t+30, the second between t+30 and t+60, the third t+60 and t+80, and the final pitch taking place between t+80 and t+100.

T+108 to MECO: this is the first part of the guided flight. The guidance system will control the missile along one of a number of alternative flight paths. All the guidance wishes to do is to get the missile to a point in space with the correct velocity so that it will reach the target in the time remaining. The guidance will endeavour to do this as smoothly and as quickly as possible. It is the conflicting requirements of small steering corrections, and shortest correcting flight path, which produces the alternative flight path situation. There are a number of alternative flight paths in space and the guidance is continuously assessing all the factors to select the one that is the most convenient.

MECO to VECO: the main engine is cut out and the final delicate adjustments are made using the vernier engines only. This is mainly so that the effects of decaying thrust will not affect the missile at the critical point when the correlated velocity is reached. This is the second portion of the guided flight.

Pre-arm: at a pre-determined point in the flight path, the operational flight safety system, a flight fail-safe arming system, will forward an arming signal to the warhead.

VECO: when the final delicate adjustments have been made to the missile's velocity, resulting in the achievement of Vc, the vernier engines are cut out.

Free flight: the missile is now in free flight and is, once again, unguided as there is no longer any need (or possibility) of influencing the flight path. Correlated velocity has been achieved and the flight path is now the true ballistic flight path.

Separation: a signal will be generated that results in the firing of the payload latch squibs, which will sever the physical attachment of the re-entry vehicle to the missile fuselage. The missile and RV possess the same velocity and, for the moment, continue together. Firing of the two ARL (Army Research Laboratory) solid-propellant retro-rockets retards the missile body, which will burn up on re-entry to the Earth's atmosphere, leaving the re-entry vehicle to continue the ballistic flight path alone, reaching the target position at t+15 minutes.

Re-Entry Vehicle (RV)

The re-entry vehicle, or nose cone, was mated to the missile at Station 42, the forward end of the guidance section. It is mostly hidden away out of sight, the only visible element of the vehicle being the somewhat curious blunt shape of the heat shield. However, it must be remembered that the RV and the payload it contained was, of course, the sole reason for the very existence of the missile; its purpose being to transport the RV to that point in space from which it would continue its journey alone back into the earth's atmosphere and onward to its intended target.

Thor was designed, at least in part, to accommodate this RV. The punishing schedule that was required to see Thor rise from the drawing boards of the Douglas Aircraft Company design offices and onto sixty launching pads scattered across the countryside of eastern England demanded as much commonality of technology with other systems that already existed (or were being developed in parallel) that it was possible to achieve. This RV (the General Electric (GE) Mk 2) was originally intended for Atlas, the first ICBM.

The blunt shape of the nose cone came about from much painstaking research, which yielded the possibly surprising result that is now so characteristic of Thor's final form.

Upon encountering the Earth's atmosphere during re-entry, the friction between the atmosphere and a returning vehicle presents an enormous problem to those tasked with the vehicle's design. This problem is one of heat, tremendous amounts of heat. Heat that must be dissipated as the vehicle decelerates in the atmosphere in order to ensure its survival. It was not until the early 1950s that scientists and engineers, among them Werner von Braun, began to consider how they could actually achieve the safe recovery to Earth of a vehicle from space. von Braun had originally considered very large vehicles with sophisticated cooling techniques that would return astronauts from space voyages, but, clearly, this would not be a solution for smaller vehicles such as those that carried the first dogs and primates into space and for the vehicle of interest here, the military missile RV.

It would seem an almost obvious choice to design a re-entry vehicle with a long, slender, pointed nose and a narrow profile in order for it to slip along in the atmosphere as easily as possible; it was in this area that early research work concentrated. When research progressed onto the testing phase, a most surprising feature of this design concept appeared. So much heat was generated that clearly a vehicle of this type would not survive the rigours of re-entry.

Scientist H. Julian Allen of the National Advisory Committee for Aeronautics (NACA, later NASA) was involved in research at the Ames Aeronautical Laboratory, addressing the issue of re-entry vehicle heat dissipation. During 1951, he discovered that rather than the sharply pointed nose that had originally been envisaged, surprisingly promising results were being yielded by a much flatter nose design. Allen and fellow scientist Alfred J. Eggars termed the vehicles of such design as 'blunt body'. The degree of protection afforded for the vehicle and its contents by the blunt-body design was far greater than had previously been achieved. This discovery was immediately classified as a military secret, but its details were published in 1958, no doubt as vehicle technology had moved on apace and more efficient designs had overtaken the original research.

The blunt-body vehicle formed a thick shockwave ahead of the vehicle, allowing a greater deceleration rate and at the same time deflecting much of the heat.

Shockwaves, or shocks, are a phenomenon affecting bodies moving at supersonic speed. A body moving through the air causes pressure waves ahead of and behind it. The faster the body moves, the more bunched up the waves ahead of the body become. At supersonic speeds, the disturbances caused by the vehicle in the air (which can only be propagated at the local speed of sound (given by the formula $38.94\sqrt{T}$ where 'T' is the absolute temperature) and which itself is influenced by the passage of the vehicle through the air) bunch up tightly and form into a V-shaped wake that is attached to the vehicle. This V-shaped wave is a shockwave. The shockwave attached to a supersonic aircraft is responsible for the sonic boom that observers hear as the aircraft passes by.

The measure of how easily a body slips through the atmosphere is determined by a formula that takes into account the mass of the vehicle, its cross section, and the drag (resistance to motion through the air) it produces. The result of this calculation is termed the ballistic coefficient (β) (beta). Re-entry vehicles, which pass through the air very readily, are termed as high-beta, while those that have high drag and consequently pass through the atmosphere relatively slowly are low-beta vehicles.

The sharply pointed vehicles originally researched are high-beta vehicles and these decelerate very little in the higher layers of the atmosphere, leaving this until the thicker, lower layers. As a result, these vehicles experience a very large amount of heating, although this is for a relatively short period. The blunt-body vehicles, conversely, are low-beta and do not penetrate the atmosphere as quickly. These vehicles experience most of their deceleration forces in the thin, higher layers of the atmosphere. Although the low-beta vehicles generate less heat, they decelerate somewhat more slowly in the thin upper air and so are subjected to the heat generated for a greater period of time.

It is not just the shape of the forward part of the vehicle that needs to be considered during the design phase, however, as the shape of the after body is also highly influential in its re-entry characteristics. There are several basic shapes available to designers of aeroshells, as the complete vehicle is often known. Of these shapes, the sphere-cone design, a spherical section, with a frustum (a cone shape cut to a blunt end) at the rear, offers some advantages over a complete sphere or a spherical section fore body, with a convergent cone shaped after body as it tends to be much more stable. The designers look carefully at the angle between the cone's axis of rotational symmetry and its outer surfaces. Half of this angle made by the cone's surface edges is a value known as simply a half-angle. With a sufficiently small half-angle and a correctly placed centre of mass, a sphere cone vehicle can be aerodynamically stable from re-entry to impact with its target.

The GE Mk 2 RV was a product of the blunt-body research and was therefore a low-beta vehicle. It was also the original American sphere-cone aeroshell.

Although the already discussed shockwave would dissipate a large proportion of the heat generated during re-entry, superheated plasma formed in front of the RV and the heat so generated found its way onto the surface of the nose of the vehicle, causing unacceptable temperature rises. Despite this advance in bringing the problem of re-entry heating under control, further measures would be required. The nose cone would need to be provided with a protective layer of material to dissipate the heat. There were two available solutions to the problem at this time, an ablative coating (which would cover the nose of the vehicle and absorb heat, charring in the process and either vaporising or flaking off, taking a large proportion of the heat with it) or a heat sink type (which would conduct the heat from the surface of the vehicle to a material that could absorb heat very readily). The major challenge here is to conduct heat away from the surface quickly enough to avoid the melting of the surface material itself.

It was this second option, the heat sink, which the USAF elected to employ on the GE Mk 2 RV. The ballistic missile division of the USAF had been testing the heat sink concept using three-stage Lockheed X-17 missiles that were fitted with scale models of the heat sink nose cone. The X-17 climbed to 400,000 feet (121,914 metres) and then turned earthward again, the second and third stages firing to ensure that the missile arrived at some 50,000 feet altitude at speeds in the region of Mach 15. This simulation of re-entry conditions was close enough to the environment that would be experienced by Thor's own RV. Several types of potential heat sink materials, including cast iron, steel, beryllium, and copper, had been evaluated before concluding that the latter yielded the best overall results and was deemed to be the most certain of success. In its final form, the heat sink was a copper alloy mass situated just under the outer shell of the vehicle, the other structural components being of stainless steel.

For the formation of the copper heat sink, two dies were manufactured, each weighing some 35 tons. To form the heat sink, the copper was put between the dies and into a hydraulic press, which was capable of supplying 50,000 tons of pressure. It was reported at the time that this was the largest ever closed-die copper forging.

The Atlas ICBM was destined to re-enter the atmosphere at speeds of up to Mach 22 and so this nose cone, although it served to provide an excellent solution to a problem within the required timeframe, was somewhat overly engineered for the speeds of Thor. Later in the programme, the nose cones allocated to the Thor programme were milled to have a much thinner heat sink, saving hundreds of pounds on the launch weight.

The GE Mk 2 RV, however, did have one major disadvantage in the role for which it had been designed. Being a low-beta vehicle, it did much of its deceleration over a relatively long period of time in the thin layers of the upper atmosphere. It spent this time with a trail of ionised gas streaming behind it. This feature, it was discovered, displayed very readily on radar. This made the vehicle relatively susceptible to interception and, therefore, not ideal for weapons delivery. Some measures were taken to reduce this vulnerability, but designers began to look towards fast moving, high-beta vehicles that would be much more difficult to counter.

The following were the principle dimensions of the GE Mk 2 RV:

Diameter: 63.6 inches (161.54 cm)
Length: 62.0 inches (157.48 cm)
Weight: 1,800 pounds (816.7 kg)
Weight of the separation system: 81.5 lb (36.98 kg)

The angle of the nose cone was a 105-degree included angle with a tip radius of 12 inches (30.48 cm).

The nose cone incorporated torus (ring doughnut shaped) tanks mounted radially around the forward part of the nose cone. These tanks were pressurised during phase one of the countdown to 6,000 psi by high-pressure nitrogen, supplied from a tank situated behind the blast wall on the northern side of the UK launch emplacements. The torus tanks fed the nitrogen to the trajectory control jets around the periphery of the RV to impart spin to the vehicle after separation from the missile fuselage, in order to improve its stability during its descent to the target. The Thor weapon system had a circular error probable of 2 miles. This means that at least 50 per cent of warheads fired should land within a radius of 2 miles of the target. Some flight tests, however, produced a much greater level of accuracy.

Transport of the RV around the site and assistance in its mating to the missile was provided by a dedicated four-wheel trailer, manufactured by the Air Logistics Corporation. The trailer was a pantograph type of device, which could be raised and lowered by means of a scissors linkage, in much the same way that catering trucks can be seen being raised to the service doors of large airliners today. The vehicle carried the RV upside down in a snugly fitting cradle. For mating, the trailer was carefully aligned with the missile's centreline, and a tool, much in the form of a large electric drill, was clipped to a torque-bearing socket, driving a shaft that caused the pantograph to raise the RV to the level of the missile. The RV cradle was rotated through 90 degrees on laterally mounted pivots and the complete assembly moved rearward to engage the RV with the missile. Once engaged, three latches were secured, which would hold the RV in place until the incorporated electrically ignited squibs were fired, allowing the RV to separate from the missile in flight.

The RV had a dedicated panel, the re-entry vehicle pre-launch monitor panel, located in the right-hand side of the electrical equipment trailer. This monitored the status of the RV and warhead, indicating the serviceability, or otherwise, of key systems, such as the weapon fusing (surface or air) and warhead battery.

The RV was prepared for launch at various phases of the countdown. During phase one, a predominantly electronic and electrical phase, the nose cone was checked and prepared. Once the 28V GSE power supply came on at the start of the phase, the nose cone 'start' relay operated and the battery heater was activated. The next stage was to check the continuity of electrical circuits and battery serviceability. The RV torus tanks were pressurised from the 6,000-psi high-pressure nitrogen tank, and the service cable was disconnected. With these actions complete, a relay operated to confirm the re-entry vehicle had been checked and this in turn caused the sending of the signal 'NOSE CONE PREPARED'. This all should happen within fifteen seconds. The activity surrounding the RV now ceased while the other phases proceeded, until in phase four, the electrical phase, when target selection was checked as complete and the missile moved onto internal power. The missile shelter had already formed another link in this sequence as it moved clear of the launcher in phase two and sent a signal confirming its position on the pad. Another relay operated to prepare the battery to come on line and to complete the sequence notifying the completion of phase four. This relay operated when the authentication officer turned his key at the launch control officer's console from 'PEACE' to 'WAR'. As the countdown proceeded to its final phase (phase five), the nose cone battery activated and its heater was switched off. The battery output was checked and if all was well, the signal 'NOSE CONE AND BATTERY READY' caused the operation of a relay in the final sequence of events. In conjunction with the operation of other relays from previous phases, all links in the chain of events were now in place for the signal 'WEAPON SYS OK'. The countdown, with respect to the RV, was now complete; the missile was only a few seconds away from the engine start sequence.

Warhead

The warhead originally intended for Thor (and, incidentally, the Jupiter IRBM and the early model Atlas and Titan ICBMs) was the W-35, an early thermonuclear warhead, possessing a yield of some 1.75 megatons (equivalent to 1.75 million tons of TNT); it was produced by the Los Alamos Scientific Laboratory. A close competitor of the W-38 warhead developed by the University of California Radiation Laboratory, the W-35 was cancelled in August 1958 in favour of a modified version of the Mk 28 bomb. The result of these modifications was the W-49 warhead, the weapon fitted to the combat configured Thors based in the UK.

The W-49 was a thermonuclear warhead, the principle statistics of which were a width of 20 inches, height of 54.3 to 57.9 inches, weight of 1,640 to 1,680 lb (depending on the model), with a yield of 1.44 megatons. It featured selectable airburst or contact fusing. It was manufactured from September 1958 to 1964, although W-49 warheads remained on the United States Air Force inventory until April 1975.

The W-49 used in THOR, incorporated several modifications in adapting the Mk 28 bomb, which included a new arming and fusing system, PAL-A. PAL (an acronym for permissive action link) is a physical component of a warhead, its function being to prevent the unauthorised activation of the weapon. In its simplest form, PAL was a four-digit combination lock, with no single individual knowing the full combination. It would therefore require two or more people (most likely two), who each knew only their particular digits. PAL became increasingly sophisticated and the version 'A' (hence, PAL-A) on the W-49 was reported to be a four-digit, ten-position electromechanical coded switch. It is generally accepted that it operated as a switching device in the high voltage circuits required for the detonation of the weapon. PAL, therefore, required a positive and deliberate human intervention in order to begin the arming process. In *Technology and the Limitation of International Conflict*, an anonymous designer was reported to have stated, somewhat colourfully, that the procedure required to defeat the PAL system protecting a weapon should be on the same level of difficulty as a surgeon removing the tonsils by entering the patient from the wrong end.

There were other measures in place to prevent arming of the weapon due to forces of nature or other accidental means. The nose cone electrical supply was separate to that for the missile, with the nose cone battery not activated until a late stage in the launch countdown sequence—after the authentication officer's key had been turned from 'PEACE' to 'WAR'. There were, however, reports that lightning strikes on a Jupiter launch site in Italy had resulted in the activation of the nose cone batteries.

Further arming of the weapon would occur during flight, typically on receipt of a signal generated by the flight control system at a pre-determined point in the missile's trajectory.

Until all elements of the arming sequence were met, it would not be possible for an accidental nuclear detonation to occur, for instance, on the launch emplacement. A spectacular example of this occurred on 25 July 1962, when the launch of a Thor from Johnston Island, as part of the Bluegill Prime high-altitude nuclear tests, failed after engine start due to a sticking valve. The range safety officer (RSO) destroyed the missile using the destruct system, while the Thor was still on the pad. The missile exploded, but there was no nuclear detonation. However, the destruction of the warhead caused extensive contamination and it became necessary to subject the entire area to a lengthy decontamination process.

The missile in this event was destroyed by the on-board self-destruct device (not present on UK combat-configured Thors), but the detonation of conventional explosives, either by accident or tampering with the weapon, was always a possibility. This type of explosion may itself lead to the release of radioactive contamination, but not to the full nuclear detonation. Procedures for eventualities such as this were practised routinely at Thor sites. The ORB, Form 540, for 106 Squadron at Bardney, reported the following practice fire exercise on launch emplacement 20, 6 May 1963, just nine days before the squadron stood down from its vigil with Thor.

Time	Condition
0920	Fire on Launch Emplacement 20.
0929	Missile engulfed in flames.
0930	Hemswell Special Safety Team Alerted.
0931	Launch Emplacement 20 evacuated.
0937	Explosion on Launch Emplacement 20. 'TOADY' reported.
0950	Site evacuated. Monitoring team formed at guardroom.
0952	2 injured casualties reported. 2 reported missing, presumed dead.
0958	Perimeter track reported clear to LE21.
1001	Radioactive contamination reported at LE20.
1046	VHF contact established with Special Safety Team.
1105	Special Safety Team on location—moving into action.
1118	Casualties located and removed.
1120	Area clear of radioactivity.
1135	Exercise complete.

Conventional weapons contain high explosives, which, upon detonation, release their energy as a result of the chemical changes experienced. Nuclear weapons, on a weight for weight basis, release vastly greater amounts of energy, which is derived from the nucleus of each atom. The yield of a nuclear weapon is so great that to compare its power in terms of the weight of an equivalent number of high explosives (TNT), it needs to be expressed in the thousands of tons (kilotons—kt) or millions of tons (megatons—mt).

Nuclear weapons release their energy by the processes of either fission or fusion. The fission weapon splits the atoms of certain elements and is limited (limited being a relative term with regard to the destructive power they can produce) by the fact that above a certain size a mass of fissile material becomes self-disruptive. The fusion weapon employs the process of fusing the nuclei of two atoms to form one, heavier atom. The nuclei of two hydrogen isotopes, deuterium and tritium, readily fuse at extremely high temperatures, and in so doing, cause the release of vast amounts of energy. These weapons require a fission device to initiate the detonation and are sometimes referred to as fission-fusion, or, more commonly, thermonuclear weapons. Fusion is a relatively clean process, the residual radiation coming from the fission products vaporised during the detonation. Thermonuclear weapons can, however, be made to produce a much larger quantity of fission products as fallout contamination by containing the device in a heavy casing of fissile material. Theoretically, thermonuclear weapons are only limited in their size by the intended method of delivery.

Thor's W-49 warhead was reported to be of a Teller-Ulam design, taking its name from the two scientists generally accepted to be its inventors. Edward Teller, who became known as the 'father' of the hydrogen bomb, had been struggling to find a solution to problems in the design of the fusion element of the device, when a Polish *émigré* mathematician, Stanislav Ulam, suggested an approach that would eventually result in the production of the first workable hydrogen device. This was tested on the island of Elugelab in the Enewetak atoll, approximately 600 nautical miles north-west of the Marshall Islands, at 7.15 a.m. local time on 1 November 1952, in an operation known as 'Ivy Mike'. The test produced a yield of 10.4 megatons, which is comparable to somewhere in the region of 500 times the yield of the 'Fat Man' bomb dropped over Nagasaki in August 1945. Upon detonation, the island disappeared, the remaining crater measuring some 6,240 feet (1.9 km) in diameter and 164 feet (50 m) deep.

The device used a fission bomb (primary) to trigger the secondary fusion part of the weapon, one 'fuel' for which was liquid deuterium, which required some 20 tons of cryogenic equipment to keep it in its liquid state. The overall weight of the device was some 80 tons and was nicknamed 'Sausage' because of the shape of some of its components. Clearly, this device would never serve as a weapon, simply because of its complexity, and the sheer size and weight involved would render it undeliverable.

The test, however, was a success and proved the concept of employing separated primary and secondary parts of the device (Stanislav Ulam's approach). The problem now was to develop the design into a small, relatively simple, lightweight package that could be delivered by air.

In developing a viable thermonuclear weapon, which would be small, simple, and lightweight, solutions had to be provided to the issues that caused the Ivy Mike device to be such a leviathan.

The basic problems were that the deuterium and tritium fuels were both gases, which raised the problems of storage. Tritium (a radioactive isotope of hydrogen) was in worldwide short supply and also has a short half-life of 12.32 years. This would mean that the tritium in the weapon would need to be constantly replenished. Another issue was that the deuterium and tritium needed to be highly compressed at extremely high temperatures, somewhere in the order of 100 million degrees Celsius, to achieve the fusion process.

In attempting to solve the issue of the deuterium gas, it was discovered that the deuterium could be chemically combined with lithium to form lithium-deuteride, a solid compound that, while it reacted in the same way as the gas, was easy to store. This would then be employed as the principal thermonuclear material in the weapon. Lithium again came to the designer's rescue in the solution to the tritium issue. Lithium, when bombarded with neutrons from a fission reaction, produced tritium. Therefore, the issues associated with the tritium were solved; before the weapon detonated, there was no tritium in the weapon that would require replenishment. Tritium was manufactured as a result of the fission reaction and was instantly ready for use in the fusion part of the process. Fission also provided the solution to the issue of the high-temperature compression of the deuterium and tritium. Most of the radiation produced by fission is in the form of X-rays, and these are the source of the temperature and pressure that are required to initiate the fusion process.

The following text gives a basic overview of the possible design and operation of this type of weapon.

Contained within the casing of the warhead is a fission (implosion) type device. This device is the primary and is required to trigger the fusion reaction. Also inside the casing, but separate from the primary, is the secondary (fusion) component of the weapon. The secondary is a cylinder of uranium 238, known as a tamper. Contained within this cylinder is the lithium-deuteride compound that surrounds, at the cylinder centre, a hollow rod of plutonium 239. This hollow plutonium rod is often referred to as the spark plug. The primary and secondary devices are separated by a shield of uranium 238, the vacant space in the warhead casing being filled by plastic foam.

When the warhead detonates, the following chain of events is set in motion:
The primary device detonates, producing intense X-ray radiation.

The X-rays cause heating of the interior of the casing and the uranium tamper, the shield acting to prevent any premature detonation of the fuel inside.

The heat produced causes burning and expansion of the tamper, which, in turn, applies pressure inwards against the lithium-deuteride, resulting in approximately a thirty-fold compression of the fuel.

Shock waves caused by the compression initiate the fission process in the plutonium 239 spark plug, which produces radiation, heat, and neutrons.

The neutrons penetrate the lithium-deuteride and combine with the lithium to produce tritium.

The extremely high temperatures and pressures achieved cause deuterium-deuterium and tritium-deuterium fusion reactions to occur and this produces more heat, radiation, and neutrons.

Neutrons released by the fusion process causes fission in the pieces of uranium 238 remaining from the tamper and the shield, which produces more heat and radiation.

Detonation.

It is reported that this entire chain of events is completed within about 600-billionths of a second, the first 550 of those billionths for the fission device to do its work and the remaining 50 billionths of the second for the fusion processes to occur. The result is an explosion of near unimaginable proportions, the results of which are discussed below.

A fireball forms at the moment of detonation. The roughly spherical mass of hot, incandescent gases rises and changes its shape due to friction with the surrounding air. The size of the fireball, the speed at which it rises, and the height to which it ascends depend largely on the power of the weapon. The surface of the fireball cools by a process of energy radiation, and it forms a violent, swirling, annular vortex. The vortex sucks air into its centre, creating the after winds and cooling itself. The speed of the swirling slows down as it cools, and may stop completely later. The vaporised parts of the weapon and other materials condense out onto dust particles. The white-hot vortex core changes colour to yellow, then red, finally losing all visible incandescence. As further cooling takes place, the main bulk of the cloud grows as atmospheric moisture condenses, forming the characteristic mushroom cloud. As the cloud ascends, it cools, reducing its buoyancy and therefore its rate of ascent. For a weapon of the size carried by Thor, detonated at the surface, the bottom of the mushroom cloud would be expected to be at a height of around 36,000 feet or so, with its top around 65,000 feet.

The distribution of radiation in the mushroom cloud varies as a function of the yield of the weapon, type of weapon, fusion/fission ratio, burst altitude, terrain type, and weather. Generally, it can be said that lower-yield explosions have about 90 per cent of radioactivity in the mushroom head and 10 per cent in the stem. Megaton-range detonations tend to have most of the radioactivity in the lower third of the mushroom cloud.

The effects of the detonation can vary widely, depending upon the weapon fusing, its power, and whether the burst was intended to be on or near the ground, in shallow water (such as a lake or harbour), in deep water out at sea, or high in the air.

For each power of weapon, there is a critical height, above which the fireball will not touch the ground. Such a burst would not produce an appreciable contamination of the ground below it or a significant fallout hazard. For a weapon of 1.44 megatons, this critical height would be in the region of 3,000 feet.

A ground-burst is a detonation that occurs either on the surface itself or below the critical height, to the extent that an appreciable part of the fireball comes into direct contact with the ground below it. As the fireball rises, it carries a large amount of vaporised materials along with it, and the winds caused as the air flows into the vortex behind it will be in the region of 200 miles per hour (320 kph). This wind will carry very large volumes of dust and other debris that will provide the medium onto which the fission products can condense. The radioactive particles that result will eventually return to the ground as fallout. The larger particles and heavier pieces of debris will fall close to the detonation site, but the smaller and lighter particles would be carried to much higher altitudes and have a slower rate of descent, significantly increasing the distance over which they travel before reaching ground level.

A water-burst is a detonation that occurs below the critical height in or over shallow or deep water. If the water is shallow, such as in a lake or river, mud and water will be vaporised and this will condense out into radioactive rain. The pattern of fallout produced will possess a smaller footprint than that of the ground burst, but the radioactivity present will be much more intense. A burst in deep water will produce similar results, with the exception of the mud particles. A higher proportion of the total energy produced will be expended in vaporising water and this will form a shock wave, which will travel out through the water, producing surface waves. A high percentage of the fission products will remain in the water near to the burst site and will be rapidly dispersed.

An airburst is a detonation that occurs above the critical height, in which case the fireball remains clear of the ground. There will be few dust particles available for the fission products to adhere to and, in general, these will be so light that a wide dispersal will take place before they reach the ground. There is no significant fallout hazard associated with an airburst.

The release of energy from a detonation at or near ground level has a rough distribution of 45 per cent as blast and shock waves; 35 per cent as light and heat radiation; 5 per cent as initial nuclear radiation; and 15 per cent as residual radiation from the fission products.

A nuclear detonation that occurs on or near the ground creates a crater and a shockwave is transmitted through the ground, radiating away from the point of detonation. As has been described, huge amounts of vaporised material and debris are sucked up into the vortex left by the rising fireball, but an even greater mass

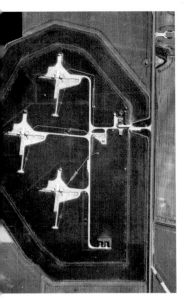

Above left: RAF Coleby Grange. (*Historic England (RAF photography)*)

Above right: RAF Folkingham. (*Historic England (RAF photography)*)

An interesting study showing the new site road laid over the existing taxiway.
(*Courtesy of Sqn Ldr W. A. Young*)

Squadron headquarters: approaching the site entrance. (*Author's Collection*)

Above: The headquarters building photographed from inside the site. This building was levelled by means of a progressively raised platform. (*Author's Collection*)

Below: The fire tender garage at Bardney. (*Author's Collection*)

Fire tender garage. Note the POL store and LCA fuel bund to the left and the site fencing to the right. (*Author's Collection*)

Above: The MEP building at Bardney. To the right of the building are the supports and concrete bund for the site standby generator fuel tank. (*Author's Collection*)

Below: A rear view of the MEP building at Bardney. (*Author's Collection*)

Above left: The classified storage building at Harrington. (*Author's Collection*)

Above right: The pyro store at Harrington. (*Author's Collection*)

The POL store at Bardney, with, at left, the bund and supports for the generator vans' fuel tank. (*Author's Collection*)

Bardney POL store. (*Author's Collection*)

Type 4 officer's married quarter in a village location, close to the Bardney Thor site. It was a 2.7-mile (4.35-km) journey from door to door. (*Author's Collection*)

Thor production line. The guidance access doors can be clearly seen. The Thor at left front has received its guidance pallet. (*RAF Museum PO15251*)

Thor production. This view shows the main engine 'bell', verniers, gas generator exhaust extension, and launch pin sockets. (*RAF Museum PO15250*)

The XLR–79 engine. (*Author's Collection*)

The turbopump assembly. (*Author's Collection*)

The complete engine. (*Author's Collection*)

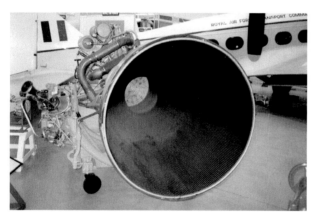

Left: Thrust chamber interior detail. (*Author's Collection*)

Below: The LR–101 vernier engine. (*Author's Collection*)

Above: The airborne guidance package. The right-hand unit shows the gimbal system with the missile guidance pallet to the left. (*Courtesy Paul O. Larson*)

Below: Pad 9 at Tuddenham photographed in the summer of 1963 as Thor's role in our nuclear deterrent came to an end. (*TNA AIR 27/2964*)

Looking up-range at the launch emplacement. (*Author's Collection*)

Above: A newly constructed shelter in its retracted position. (*Author's Collection*)

Left: This study of technicians at work in the shelter shows the access afforded by the flight controller and guidance section work stands. (*IWM (RAF–T881)*)

27 A Thor on its transporter/erector with an M52 tractor unit, behind which can be clearly seen the Douglas ring on the nose of the missile. (*Author's Collection*)

Thor rear steersman. This driver had control of the front set of dolly wheels and his headset is clearly in evidence. (*Author's Collection*)

A Thor threading its way through a Northamptonshire village. (*USAF*)

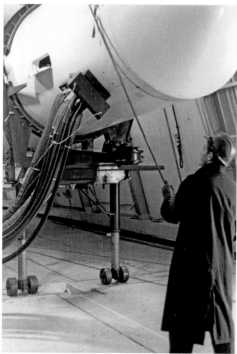

Above: The launch mounting during an erecting cycle. The air conditioning and RP-1 feed pipe geometry are clearly visible. (*Courtesy Sqn Ldr W. A. Young*)

Left: The umbilical lines plug carrier and lanyards. (*Courtesy Sqn Ldr W. A. Young*)

An atmospheric night study, RP–1 tank and pad detail. (*IWM (RAF–T876)*)

The LOX storage tank. See text for more details. (*IWM (RAF–T875)*)

Above left: Practice countdown. (*IWM (RAF–T2615)*)

Above right: The LOX supply gallows units. (*Courtesy Sqn Ldr W. A. Young*)

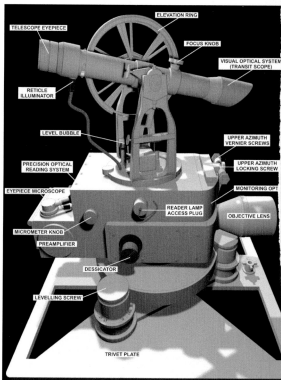

Above left: Precision AC multi-turn potentiometer. (*Author's Collection*)

Above right: Short-range theodolite. (*Tim Goodchild*)

Above: Collimator: two such units were provided on the guidance platform. (*Author's Collection*)

Below left: The guidance platform, showing an SRT and collimator. The two flaps giving optical access to the guidance are clearly visible. (*TNA. Air 27/2758*)

Below right: Target reference pillar at Harrington, *c.* 1995. (*Author's Collection*)

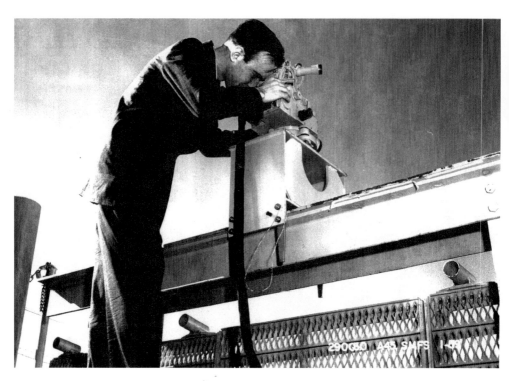

Practical demonstration of SRT set-up. (*Courtesy of Paul O. Larson*)

Scramble! Technicians depart the LCA for their launch emplacements on a practice countdown. (*Courtesy Sqn Ldr W. A. Young*)

of material is deposited around the edge of the crater to form a highly radioactive crater lip. The shock wave that radiates outwards, much like the rings that form in water when a pebble is thrown in, is similar in magnitude—for a megaton-range weapon—to a moderate earthquake. Subterranean structures and services are not likely to be affected at distances greater than 1 mile for a 5-mt weapon.

A detonation will also produce a wave of high-pressure air radiating outwards, developing into a shock front. The pressure wave is followed up by a suction wave. The wave travels at speeds in excess of the speed of sound in the initial stage, slowing down and equalling the speed of sound at a long distance from the detonation. The damage and the distance over which it is caused by the blast will depend upon the power of the weapon, the type of burst, and the size and strength of affected structures. A rough guide to the destructive power of a 1.44-mt weapon, detonated as a ground burst, would be in the order of 2 miles (3.2 km) for total destruction, 2 to 3 miles (3.2 to 4.8 km) for irreparable damage, 3 to 7 miles (4.8 to 11.4 km) for moderate damage, and slight damage expected at 7 to 12 miles (11.4 to 19.2 km).

The longevity and the physical size of the fireball produced by a detonation will depend upon the power of the weapon. The fireball from a weapon of the power of that dropped at the close of the Second World War would last in the region of one and a half seconds. The fireball from a 10-mt detonation would be expected to last for a period of about twenty seconds. The heat and light radiation can cause fires and burning of the skin at considerable range from the detonation. A 20-kt airburst detonation will produce a fire zone of some 1.5 miles (2.4 km) with isolated fires at 2 miles (3.2 km). The zones associated with a 5-mt airburst would be 15 miles (24 km) and 22 miles (35 km) respectively. The fire zones created by ground-burst detonations are smaller. Skin burns are discussed under the biological effects of the weapon.

The initial radiations include the instantaneous radiations and those that are released within the first minute after detonation. It generally consists of neutrons and gamma rays. The neutrons of the initial radiation are not considered to be hazardous, but only because the range at which they could cause damage is well within the range where the other effects of the detonation would most certainly prove lethal. It is for the same reason that the gamma rays from the initial radiation of megaton-range weapons can also be ignored. In the case of weapons in the kiloton range, however, this gamma radiation becomes a significant hazard as it possesses a range in excess of the other effects.

Residual radiation arises from the fission products of the weapon, which are vaporised by the searing heat developed within the fireball. These products then condense out in the cloud onto debris and dust and fall back to the surface, covering a wide area with radioactive fallout. As discussed later, residual radiation decays rapidly at first, but this decay slows as time progresses. It may continue to be hazardous for a very long period.

Nuclear detonations produce a fireball, which can produce flash-blindness both direct and indirect and may cause permanent damage to the eyes. During daylight, the pupil of the eye has a very small diameter; this, coupled with the reflex action to blink, should prevent burning of the retina at a distance from the detonation that is considered survivable. Indirect flash, which results from the scattering of light in clouds and the atmosphere, is not normally a problem. Protection of the eyes even during daylight, however, remains a sensible precaution. During the hours of darkness, the problems associated with the flash are much amplified and even indirect flash may render an observer at a survivable distance blind for a long period. The pupils of the eye dilate in darkness and protection of the eyes is absolutely essential during this time.

Skin burns will occur in people directly exposed to the rays from the fireball. The severity will clearly vary with distance and power of the weapon, blistering being caused by a 20-kt weapon at a range of 1.25 miles (2 km), while a 5-mt weapon would cause the same effect at some 18 miles (29 km). Light-coloured clothing tends to reflect some of the heat and light radiation of the fireball, which is the reason that the RAF's V-bombers were originally painted in overall gloss white.

The detonation of a nuclear weapon will also result in the release of different types of radiation, each possessing differing properties. They are alpha particles, beta particles, and gamma rays.

Alpha particles are fast moving particles and their ability to penetrate is somewhat limited. They are easily absorbed within a few inches of air, or even a sufficiently thick sheet of paper; therefore, they have a limited range. If these particles can be kept outside of the body, there is virtually no threat. Should microscopic alpha emitters manage to enter the body's internal systems, however, then the risk becomes significant. The most likely points of entry into the body are via open wounds, the digestive tract, or the lungs.

Beta particles move at exceptionally high speeds and possess greater penetrative power than the alpha particles. Even so, 7 to 10 feet (2 to 3 metres) of air or reasonably thick clothing will absorb them. Should beta particles make contact with an area of bare skin, external injuries in the form of lesions could be expected to appear in the course of two to three weeks, and, unless a prolonged exposure was experienced, would normally be expected to start healing after a period of approximately nine weeks. This type of injury is known as beta burning. As with the alpha particles, the main issue associated with the beta particles is from the body being subject to internal radiation after the contamination is ingested into the body.

Gamma rays pose by far the greatest hazard. They are of short wavelength and highly penetrative, even more so than X-rays, and are consequently not as easily absorbed as were the alpha and beta particles. It would require several inches of steel or several feet of wood to reduce the gamma radiation by a factor of ten.

Radiation ionizes and excites the cells of living tissue and alters or simply destroys some of the constituents of the cell that are vital to its correct functioning.

In this process, other products are formed and these can act as poisons. The degree of injury caused will depend on several factors, including the part of the body affected, how much of the body is exposed to the radiation, and the dose rate received. The parts of the body most sensitive to this type of injury are lymphoid tissue, bone marrow, the reproductive system, spleen, and the gastro-intestinal tract. The skin, liver, and the lungs are less sensitive, with bones, nerves, and the muscles showing the least sensitivity. If the exposure is of the whole body, then the injuries are widespread and any recovery will be difficult. If, however, exposure is limited, those regions of the body that remained unexposed can in fact aid the recovery of the damaged areas. The dose rate is a very important factor. If, for a given dose, the dose rate is such that the body absorbs the radiation over a long period—say, a number of years—the victim may not display any noticeable effects of the exposure. Should the same dose be administered in a very short period, it may well prove to be fatal.

Radiation decays with the passage of time and is most rapid in the initial hours after the detonation. This is because the radiation will be a mixture of fission products, some of which will decay very rapidly and some will decay very slowly. The short-lived products will soon disappear, causing the initial rapid reduction in the radioactivity level, but the slower decaying products will remain. The decay rate can be given mathematically as the 't to the minus one point two decay law', but as with many things, there is a rough 'rule of thumb' for estimating the reduction in the radiation dose rate. This is known as the seven-tenths rule (7/10). It states that as time since the detonation is multiplied by seven, the radiation dose rate divides by ten.

An example of this would be in taking 'H' hour as the time of detonation and an initial dose rate of 1,000 units per hour (usually measured in centigrays per hour), then at H+7 hours the dose rate could be expected to divide by 10 and be 100 units per hour. If we apply the rule again, it would be shown that at H+49 hours (two days) the dose rate would be reduced to 10 units per hour. As can be seen, the initial reduction in the dose rate is rapid, but then slows considerably—in the example above, it takes a further two weeks to divide by 10 once more.

It should be appreciated that all radiation is extremely harmful and its effects continue long after the initial event.

3

The Launch Emplacement

The Launch Emplacement

The emplacements were constructed from reinforced concrete with a 'dry lean' concrete sub-base (having a high aggregate to cement ratio). This was covered by 6 inches (15 cm) of high-quality concrete that was accurate in level to ⅛ inch (3 mm). Some concrete layers were vibrated. When poured normally, concrete includes irregularly distributed trapped air. Applying vibration agitates the particles within the mix and destroys the friction between them. The mix becomes unstable and, under the influence of the vibration and gravity, flows to fit the formwork containing it and snugly around the reinforcing bars. The particles in the mix are also rearranged so that the mortar drops into spaces between the aggregate, and at the same time, the air rises to the surface and is discharged. It was vital that the emplacements did not suffer any settling of the concrete as this would affect the precise levels of the emplacement and could introduce guidance alignment errors.

Each emplacement was provided with seven lighting gantries, made from steel ⅜ inch (9.5 mm) thick with a diameter of 12 inches (30.5 cm). These provided a shadow-less environment for night operations. Each gantry was equipped with a platform and ladder and it was not uncommon for this vantage point to be used by the RAF police for surveillance of the surrounding area. Some gantries were also fitted with PA loud speakers. The total length of an emplacement was in the region of 680 feet (207 metres) with a width of some 415 feet (126.5 metres).

The following pages look in detail at the launch emplacement equipment. It is interesting to note that all but 13 per cent of the total cost of the Thor weapon system was accounted for by the ground-based equipment.

Referring to the photograph looking up-range from the launch emplacement, it will be seen that, after almost half a century, a well-preserved emplacement will still reveal a good deal of detail. Closest to the camera are the pads to which the launch mounting was bolted. At the centre of this area can be seen four small, dark rectangles. Should straight lines join the opposing pairs of rectangles, the brass reference stud marking the centre of the missile (when vertical) can be distinguished at the intersection of the lines. The recessed areas to the extreme left and right in the foreground are for the LOX and RP-1 valve complexes respectively. To the right of the

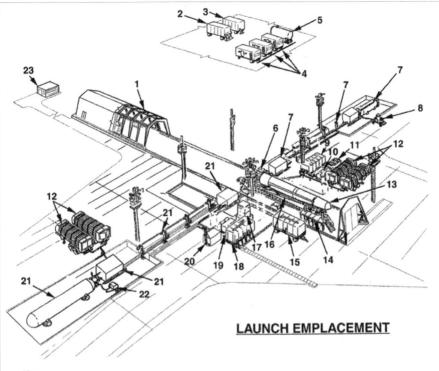

LAUNCH EMPLACEMENT

Key

1. Panelized Prefabricated Building SHU-2/E
2. Trailer-Mounted Power Switchboard JEU-2/M
3. Trailer-Mounted Launching Control Group A/M24A-2
4. Trailer-Mounted Diesel Engine Generator Set AF/M32A-12*
5. Diesel Fuel Storage Tank TMU-5/E*
6. Ballistic Missile Erecting-Launching Mount MTU-1A/E
7. Fuel Pipeline Outfit GSU-6/E and Fuel Storage Tank TMU-4/E
8. Trailer-Mounted Fuel Filter Unit GSU-7M
9. Trailer-Mounted Hydro-Pneumatic Systems Controller AF/M46A-1
10. High Pressure Gas Storage Tank TMU-6/E*
11. Power-Driven Reciprocating Compressor A/M32A-27*
12. Compressed Gas Cylinder Semitrailer AF/M32A-17 Typical (2 Places)*
13. SM-75 Missile*

14. Short Range Azimuth Alignment Electrotheodolite AN/GVQ-3
15. Trailer-Mounted Ballistic Missile System Checkout STation TTU-92/M*
16. Ballistic Missile Erecting-Transporting Boom GSU-33/E, And Rear Dolly GSU-32/M
17. Trailer-Mounted Air Conditioner AF/M32C-1*
18. Trailer-Mounted Missile Launching Countdown Group A/M24A-1A
19. Hydraulic Pumping Unit PMU-14/E
20. Skid-Mounted Power Switchboard JEU-1/E
21. Liquid Oxygen Pipeline Outfit GSU-5/E
22. Trailer-Mounted Vacuum Pump PMU-1/M
23. Long Range Azimuth Alignment Electrotheodolite AN/GVQ-4

*This Equipment Located at the Launch Emplacement and Rim Building

rearmost bolt set can be seen the hole housing the flange, where the RP-1 feed pipe to the missile emerged from the concrete, while the stainless steel flange to the left is the LOX overflow from the missile, leading into the pit (extreme left), which now provides a home to this large bush. To the left of the blue rucksack can be seen the bolts for the shelter rails (also visible on right) and just ahead of the rucksack is the anchor point for the shelter operating cable. The point for the other cable can be seen at right, in the mossy area. Just visible at the end of the pad causeway, against the tree line, is the small building that housed the long-range theodolite. The distance from the reference stud to the theodolite mounting is 425 feet (129.5 metres).

Missile Shelter

Dominating the launch emplacement was the missile shelter, a movable hangar that afforded protection from the elements for the missile, transporter/erector, launch mounting, and guidance platform, upon which the short-range theodolites were mounted. The environment within the shelter was regulated by the provided air conditioning and heating units, with the temperature generally controlled to about 21° Celsius (70° Fahrenheit). The shelter was essentially two structures, firstly an open-ended main enclosure, comprising the rear wall, sidewalls, and roof, and secondly, a freestanding front wall that provided the means of closure at the down-range end.

The shelter measured 108 feet long by 28 feet 10 inches wide and 20 feet high (32.9 × 8.8 × 6.1 metres). The structure was pre-fabricated from ten main lateral frames, which provided the basic skeleton. This was then clad by steel-covered panels containing a paper honeycomb-sandwich filling, with a thickness of some 2½ inches. The panels used were of two sizes: 8 feet (2.44 metres) and 3 feet 11 inches (1.2 metres) wide—both sizes being a length of 15 feet 7 inches (4.75 metres). The interior was well-equipped, allowing easy access to the missile, having three retractable maintenance platforms, two on the right side and one on the left. The forward-most platforms were located between the second and third shelter frames from the front. Looking down-range, the platforms on the left and right sides afforded access to the guidance pallet section and to the flight control section respectively, while the third platform allowed activity at the centre section of the missile. Suspended from 'I' beams were two hoists, each having a capacity of approximately 1,100 lb (500 kg). Other interior equipment included the essential lighting, heating, ventilation, and electrical supplies. A machine-room wall at the rear of the shelter segregated the drive motor, gearbox, and the retraction control cabinet. Warning horns were provided to alert personnel of the imminent, and continued, movement of the shelter. Outside, six floodlights assisted the overall lighting of the emplacement, and two red lights, one on the roof apex at each end, were provided as obstruction lights.

The main shelter ran along two railway type rails, bolted to each side of the launch emplacement and of some 300 feet (91.5 metres) in length. The shelter was actually free-running with respect to the rails, motive power being provided by a 60-hp electric motor, located in the machine room at the up-range end, spooling cables via a geared drive system. Two wire rope cables, each approximately 205 feet (62.5 metres) in length and of ¾ inch (19 mm) diameter, were laid along the launch emplacement parallel to, and just inboard of, the shelter rails. The cables were secured to mounting brackets located just up-range from the launch mounting and again at the rear of the launch emplacement. The shelter drive method may be easily demonstrated by taking a length of string, wrapped a few turns around a pencil held perpendicular to the line of travel, and then pulled straight and taped to a flat surface at both ends. Rotating the pencil will cause it to travel towards one end of the string. Reversing the rotation will cause travel in the opposite direction. The shelter drive system operated along this basic principle.

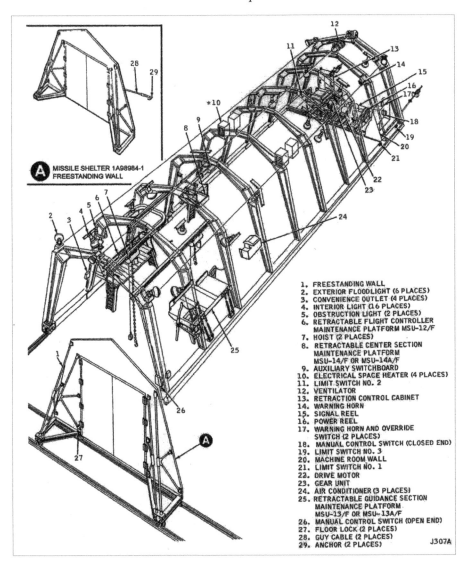

1. FREESTANDING WALL
2. EXTERIOR FLOODLIGHT (6 PLACES)
3. CONVENIENCE OUTLET (4 PLACES)
4. INTERIOR LIGHT (16 PLACES)
5. OBSTRUCTION LIGHT (2 PLACES)
6. RETRACTABLE FLIGHT CONTROLLER MAINTENANCE PLATFORM MSU-12/F
7. HOIST (2 PLACES)
8. RETRACTABLE CENTER SECTION MAINTENANCE PLATFORM MSU-14/F OR MSU-14A/F
9. AUXILIARY SWITCHBOARD
10. ELECTRICAL SPACE HEATER (4 PLACES)
11. LIMIT SWITCH NO. 2
12. VENTILATOR
13. RETRACTION CONTROL CABINET
14. WARNING HORN
15. SIGNAL REEL
16. POWER REEL
17. WARNING HORN AND OVERRIDE SWITCH (2 PLACES)
18. MANUAL CONTROL SWITCH (CLOSED END)
19. LIMIT SWITCH NO. 3
20. MACHINE ROOM WALL
21. LIMIT SWITCH NO. 1
22. DRIVE MOTOR
23. GEAR UNIT
24. AIR CONDITIONER (3 PLACES)
25. RETRACTABLE GUIDANCE SECTION MAINTENANCE PLATFORM MSU-13/F OR MSU-13A/F
26. MANUAL CONTROL SWITCH (OPEN END)
27. FLOOR LOCK (2 PLACES)
28. GUY CABLE (2 PLACES)
29. ANCHOR (2 PLACES)

J307A

A MISSILE SHELTER 1A98984-1 FREESTANDING WALL

The shelter and associated equipment. (*USAF*)

Two drums rotated with the drive to act as spools for the 480V AC electrical power feed and the intercommunication cabling.

As the shelter retracted, it left the freestanding wall in place at the down-range end of the launch emplacement. Fitted with double doors, large enough to allow a transporter/erector and its tractor unit to pass through, the wall and its supporting structure could be moved laterally, again on rails, to the left looking down-range, in order to clear the emplacement centreline.

The shelter was retracted during phase two, the mechanical phase, of the launch countdown. As this phase commenced, a shelter start signal was sent via the

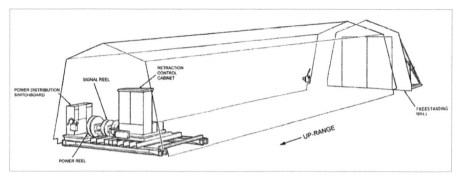

Shelter retraction drive mechanism. (*USAF*)

hydraulic pumping unit and the retraction sequence would begin, accompanied by the warning klaxon. The shelter moved initially in a low gear until its front end passed the rear of the launch mounting, when a micro switch was tripped sending a signal to indicate 'shelter removed', confirming that the shelter had retracted a distance of 93 feet (28.3 metres) and was therefore clear of the launcher. This signal, in conjunction with the successful test gimballing of the sustainer and vernier engine chambers, gave the signal to start the hydraulic pumping unit and the erector ram began to raise the missile to the vertical. Additionally, the triggering of the micro switch at the 93-foot point caused the shelter retraction drive mechanism to change into a high gear until the shelter was stowed at the up-range end of the launch emplacement. A limit switch operated at the end of shelter travel to cut out the motor drive. At the same time, a 'shelter clear' signal was sent, indicating that the shelter had now retracted 192 feet (58.5 metres) and was stowed correctly. This last signal caused the operation of a relay that was also part of the phase four sequence. Shelter removed and shelter clear lights were incorporated on the launch control console operator's malfunction panel. The LCCO panel also included a 'shelter clear' override button. Manual and override controls were also provided within the shelter.

Transporter/Erector

The missile was transported to the launch site, supported at rest in its shelter, and raised to the vertical launch position by the appropriately named transporter/ erector. When in transit to the launch site and during operations to mate the missile with the launch mount, the transporter/erector was articulated to a prime mover tractor vehicle. Initially, this was the American-supplied International Harvester M52, but, with a government anxious to utilise British equipment wherever possible for reasons of political sensitivity, this unit was later replaced by the Leyland Hippo.

The transporter/erector was produced by the Food Machinery and Chemical Corporation (FMC) of San Jose, California. FMC had been manufacturing military vehicles since 1941 and was awarded the contract for the transporter/erector, launch mounting, and the hydraulic pumping unit in January 1957; the first production equipment was delivered to Douglas in September of the same year, two months ahead of schedule.

The transporter/erector incorporated forward and aft cradles. The forward cradle possessed clamshell arms, which secured the missile circumferentially and coincided with the substantial bulkhead immediately behind the guidance section at Station 151. The missile was transported without its re-entry vehicle in place, and therefore some 9 feet 1 inch (2.77 metres) of the airframe protruded forward of the clamshells. When in transit, a device known as the 'Douglas Ring' was fitted to the open forward end of the airframe to provide continuous essential supplies, such as power for the gyro heating, to the guidance system. The clamshell system also included a device for closing the door that afforded the short-range theodolites optical access to the guidance system. The rear cradle supported the missile's lower end at approximately Station 600 and could be raised or lowered by means of two hydraulic jacks to ensure precise missile alignment to the launcher. Knurled adjustment nuts could then be set to maintain the position. During transit, two triangular travel locks were bolted to the transporter

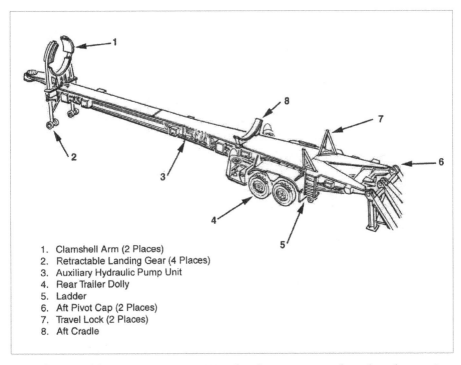

1. Clamshell Arm (2 Places)
2. Retractable Landing Gear (4 Places)
3. Auxiliary Hydraulic Pump Unit
4. Rear Trailer Dolly
5. Ladder
6. Aft Pivot Cap (2 Places)
7. Travel Lock (2 Places)
8. Aft Cradle

Major features of the transporter/erector. Note that the transporter to lower launch mounting mating detail is shown. (*USAF*)

deck, securing the Thor and supporting the weight of the heavy engine and accessories section by means of bolts passing through the top mountings of the locks into launch pin sockets number two and number six in the missile's base plate.

For transporting the missile, a detachable four-wheel dolly, featuring two pairs of wheels in tandem, were provided at the rear of the transporter/erector and supported approximately 70 per cent of the weight of the missile and transporter combination, the remaining 30 per cent being borne by the attachment to the tractor unit. The dolly was attached in three places to the transporter/erector. Mountings attached to the transporter main structure fitted to the dolly lower frame between each pair of tandem wheels. They were fixed with suspension pins, these being safety pinned after fitting to ensure their retention. Forward mounting was achieved via means of a lunette eye and screw that affixed into a locknut assembly on the transporter. Once the transporter/erector was attached to the launch mounting, the rear dolly unit was removed, although some photographs, including one in this book, do show an erect missile with the unit still in place.

Initially, the design of the transporter called for the rear wheels to be fixed in the direction of travel; however, late in 1957, it was realised that this arrangement would not be suitable for negotiating the winding nature of the roads of rural England. A trailer of some 64 feet (19.5 metres) in length, with fixed rear axles, would, necessarily, cut across corners and travel a considerable distance before the tractor-trailer combination was once again aligned. Even if it had been possible to do this in open countryside, which was by no means guaranteed, the villages through which Thor would inevitably have to pass, with buildings on corner locations, would preclude this. The rear dolly was therefore modified to provide the wheels with a steering capability. At the forward end of each pair of wheels, a steering cockpit was installed, incorporating a seat (with seat belt, fortunately) and a steering wheel. The structure of the cockpit was a simple platform with a vertical surface and windscreen providing a small measure of protection for the occupant, known as a rear steersman. This new vehicle configuration was tested in secrecy at the Moffet Federal Airfield, some 7 miles to the north west of San Jose. The transporter/erector now had a crew of three who needed to work in a highly coordinated manner. To that end, the rear steersmen and the tractor unit driver were connected by an intercom system through headsets. The provision of two rear steersmen offered the transporter crew a choice of steering combinations, ideal for the conditions to be found in the UK; the steersman on the right-hand side operated the front pair of wheels and the other, on the left, the rear set. The wheel sets could thus be operated as required to achieve the necessary manoeuvrability in limited space situations and to achieve alignment of the tractor unit and trailer as quickly as possible with minimum cutting of the corners. During such operations, the rear steersmen were in charge, and via the intercom system, kept the tractor unit driver advised as to the speed required. Generally, in tight situations, this was no more than 5 mph. Despite the addition of the steerable dolly, there remained a requirement for a certain physical easing of the bends in the roads at some locations between the main bases and the dispersed launch sites. By the positioning of lock pins provided at the steering position, selections could be made to have no rear steering, manual steering, or power-assisted (pneumatic) steering.

Referring to the photograph of the Thor threading its way through a village in transit to the launch site, the pairs of rear wheels can be seen assisting the transporter back into alignment with the tractor unit. Also visible are the guide pin and brackets, which were provided at the rear of the transporter for the alignment and attachment respectively of the vehicle to the launch mounting during the mating procedure. It was about these attachments that the transporter would pivot during the erection of the missile to the vertical. These features will be described later in the text.

The transporter/erector was equipped with retractable landing gears, identical to those that can be seen on the trailers of articulated lorries today. The forward end of the transporter had one pair of landing gears attached to the lower mounting of the clamshell supports, an identical set being provided at the rear immediately behind the dolly wheels. The gear units were operated by use of a ratchet handle that featured a selectable switch. In the 'on' position, operation of the ratchet handle extended the gear, while operation with the switch to the 'off' position would retract the gear. In addition to the switch, the ratchet handle head could be pushed in or pulled out on its input shaft, as appropriate, to change the gearing and hence the speed of gear extension or retraction. With the shaft selected to the innermost position, the gearing was at a low speed setting, a high-speed setting being achieved by pulling the input shaft to the outermost position. The landing wheels themselves were castors, but they could be locked by inserting a locking knob into a detent. The landing gears supported the transporter/erector when it was attached to the launch mounting, although the forward landing gears could be used in the conventional sense when the transporter/erector was not attached to its tractor unit.

An auxiliary hydraulic pump unit was located on the left-hand side of the transporter/erector. It included three hand pumps, one for the clamshells that, through using open and close pushbuttons controlling a valve, would perform both functions, and one for each of the rear cradle jacks. The system capacity was 6 quarts of hydraulic fluid and each hand pump had an associated pressure gauge. There were two pressure release valves for the aft cradle, to allow for the lowering of an elevated cradle.

Launch Mounting

The launch mounting was a substantial two-part structure, comprising a lower mounting, bolted to the launch emplacement, and an upper mounting, hinged at its forward edge to the lower. This arrangement was dictated by the necessity of transporting and storing the missile in the horizontal and launching it from the vertical. The position of the launch mounting was referenced to a brass stud, set into the launch emplacement concrete and which would be exactly under the

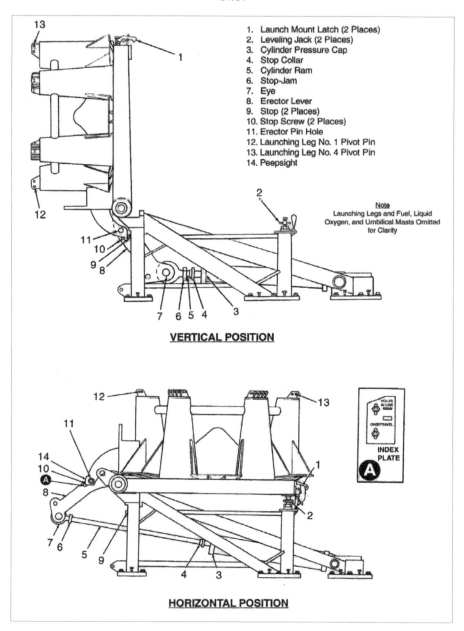

1. Launch Mount Latch (2 Places)
2. Leveling Jack (2 Places)
3. Cylinder Pressure Cap
4. Stop Collar
5. Cylinder Ram
6. Stop-Jam
7. Eye
8. Erector Lever
9. Stop (2 Places)
10. Stop Screw (2 Places)
11. Erector Pin Hole
12. Launching Leg No. 1 Pivot Pin
13. Launching Leg No. 4 Pivot Pin
14. Peepsight

Note
Launching Legs and Fuel, Liquid
Oxygen, and Umbilical Masts Omitted
for Clarity

VERTICAL POSITION

INDEX
PLATE

HORIZONTAL POSITION

Major components of the launch mounting. (*USAF*)

centre of the engine bell with the missile vertical. Operations to raise and lower the missile were enabled by having the transporter/erector attached by pivot points to the lower launch mounting. To complete the launch mounting equipment, an umbilical mast was provided to supply services to missile systems. The hydraulic pumping unit provided hydraulic power and electrical control signals.

The lower launch mounting, precisely engineered from welded steel sections, was bolted to the launch emplacement in five locations. The mounting consisted of four main legs and a rear unit, which was attached to the forward upper part of the structure by two heavy beams. It provided the attachment point for the erector cylinder, which contained the hydraulic ram utilised to raise and lower the missile and transporter/erector combination. The ram was reputed to be capable of providing over 100 tons of thrust. A specially engineered packaged valve assembly, produced by Vickers Incorporated of Waterbury, Connecticut, provided control of the erector cylinder. Its design achieved regulated acceleration and deceleration in the erecting cycle without compounding structural vibration. Vickers also produced the control valves for the launch mount masts. The front legs of the launch mounting were each bolted to a square pad in four places, while basically rectangular pads, carrying six bolts each, secured the rear legs. A further ten bolts held down the ram attachment unit, making for a total of thirty bolts. In service, the ram attachment mount was covered by a set of steps affording access to the launch mounting. The forward edge of the lower launch mounting incorporated four lugs to which the upper launch mounting was hinged and also provided the pivot points around which the transporter/erector would be raised and lowered. The mounting also provided pivot points for an erector lever and its associated link, levelling jacks, an electrical junction box, and a hydraulic manifold.

The construction of the upper launch mounting was identical to that of the lower unit. The central feature of the upper mounting was the cone-shaped flame deflector, its rounded apex positioned directly in line with the engine nozzle, designed to deflect the inferno of the rocket engine's exhaust down and away from the missile as protection against blast damage. It was also important to minimise the effects of heat and blast damage on surrounding support equipment, at least until the moment of launch. Some launch emplacement cabling and connectors were laid inside conduit-type covered trenches, while equipment and associated cabling surrounding the launch mounting or connected to the missile itself were afforded a measure of protection by the application of a urethane based compound that was nicknamed 'Pucky'. This ablative material was only temporary protection, however, lasting long enough to see the missile launched, after which the equipment and cabling would be destroyed by the combined actions of the heat and blast. As UK-based launch emplacements were never intended to support multiple firings, post-launch destruction of support equipment was not going to be an issue.

Equally spaced around the circumference of the flame deflector were six fixed support pylons, approximately 5 feet (1.5 metres) in height; hinged to the top of each was a retractable launching leg of similar dimension, equipped with a hydraulic actuator that could pivot the leg in an outward direction away from the missile. The legs were retracted for mating operations and at missile lift-off. The launching legs were numbered, number one at the bottom centre (with the launcher horizontal) and numbering clockwise when facing down-range. With the missile in place, the open end of the engine bell was approximately in line with the launching legs hinge line. Holding the missile at this height ensured sufficient ground clearance for effective engine operation and protection. The upper mount also carried the RP-1 fuel supply pipe, its quick release coupling and associated actuator, the liquid oxygen mast structure assembly, which supported the quick release LOX supply pipe and its hydraulic actuator, the upper portion of the erector lever, and the guide plate for aligning the transporter/erector during mating with the launch mounting. The right-hand side of the upper launch mounting (facing down-range) provided the attachment points for an umbilical mast, approximately 60 feet (18.3 metres) in length, in the form of a lattice tower.

The umbilical tower provided the required services and signalling up to the moment of launch. The services included air conditioning for the guidance compartment, guidance pallet, inverter, inlet and outlet air of the air measurement unit, and signals for the guidance set and re-entry vehicle. A relatively short fly-lead arrangement carried the services from the top of the mast and terminated on the umbilical lines plug carrier, which plugged into a receptacle in the missile's nose, just forward of the short-range theodolite access door. The plug carrier was a rectangular device, pivoted to which was a wedge-shaped forks arrangement. The open end of each fork supported a small wheel. The umbilical tower was hinged so that an attached hydraulic actuator could move the tower toward the missile after mating with the launcher, and allow insertion of the plug carrier. The tower would move rapidly away from the missile during launch, at which time wire lanyards, attached from the mast to the forks on the plug, caused the forks to pivot, their wheels running across the side of the missile, the lengthening of the forks forcing the disconnection of the plug carrier from the airframe, thus removing the last ties between the ground equipment and the missile, which was now autonomous.

For mating, the transporter/erector was reversed up to the launch mounting, the top portion of which was already in the horizontal to receive the missile, its launching legs retracted, allowing easy access for the engine bell. The deck of the transporter/erector split at the rear of the trailer to form an open V-shape, each arm of the 'V' terminating in an aft pivot for attachment to the launch mounting. The pivots consisted of two parts, a fixed lower part and a hinged upper part, known as a pivot cap. Fixed a little distance in from the pivots was a lateral structural member that carried a bracket supporting a vertical guide-pin. Attached to the upper launch mounting was a plate that contained a wedge-shaped cut-out terminating in a slot. As the transporter edged ever closer to the launch mounting, the vertical guide pin attached to the back of the transporter engaged with the cut-out and progressed eventually into the slot, this simple guidance system ensuring that the aft pivot points of the transporter would be in perfect alignment with their counterparts on the launch mounting. As the transporter's aft pivot points were positioned directly under the launch mounting pivot points, its rear landing gear legs were lowered, raising the pivot points to contact the launch mounting, the hinged pivot caps then being closed and bolted to the lower points to complete the pivot. The transporter's front landing gears were deployed, the tractor unit now free to unhitch and drive away. For transit, launch pin sockets numbers two and six were occupied by travel locks, which were removed and stowed at the transporter sides, the launching legs coming back into alignment at the base plate of the missile and located by spigots. All six launch pins were then electrically driven in to secure the missile.

The erector cylinder anchored to the rear unit of the lower launch mounting achieved raising and lowering of the missile. The cylinder ram was connected to an erector lever that raised and lowered the upper launch mounting and provided the attachment point for a substantial erector link, via which the force of the hydraulic ram was applied directly to the transporter/erector for raising and lowering operations. Hinging the launch mountings and transporter/erector about the same axis ensures that the entire assembly will remain aligned at all times. A device known as a 'come along', attached to a transporter lateral structural member was employed to lift this heavy link to a pivot point

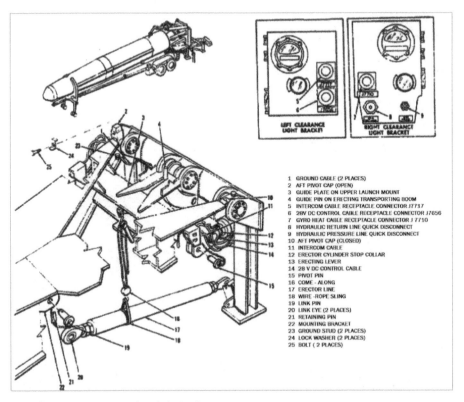

1 GROUND CABLE (2 PLACES)
2 AFT PIVOT CAP (OPEN)
3 GUIDE PLATE ON UPPER LAUNCH MOUNT
4 GUIDE PIN ON ERECTING TRANSPORTING BOOM
5 INTERCOM CABLE RECEPTACLE CONNECTOR J7717
6 28V DC CONTROL CABLE RECEPTACLE CONNECTOR J7656
7 GYRO HEAT CABLE RECEPTACLE CONNECTOR J 7710
8 HYDRAULIC RETURN LINE QUICK DISCONNECT
9 HYDRAULIC PRESSURE LINE QUICK DISCONNECT
10 AFT PIVOT CAP (CLOSED)
11 INTERCOM CABLE
12 ERECTOR CYLINDER STOP COLLAR
13 ERECTING LEVER
14 28 V DC CONTROL CABLE
15 PIVOT PIN
16 COME - ALONG
17 ERECTOR LINE
18 WIRE -ROPE SLING
19 LINK PIN
20 LINK EYE (2 PLACES)
21 RETAINING PIN
22 MOUNTING BRACKET
23 GROUND STUD (2 PLACES)
24 LOCK WASHER (2 PLACES)
25 BOLT (2 PLACES)

Launch mounting mating detail. (*USAF*)

on the centreline under the transporter. Once in place, a large pin, retained by a safety clip, functioned as the pivot. A 'come along' is simply a ratchet device that, although light in weight, assists in lifting quite heavy loads and was ideally suited to this type of operation. It would not be suitable for handling overhead loads.

Hydraulic Pumping Unit

The hydraulic pumping unit (HPU), also a product of the Food Machinery and Chemical Company, was responsible for supplying all hydraulic pressure to the launch mounting and its associated services. In addition, it supplied electrical control signals for the operation of the hydraulic control systems and, perhaps less obvious, the signals for the operation of the missile shelter and the launch pins.

The HPU centred on a 60-hp motor that powered the Vickers-built hydraulic power unit. This ported hydraulic pressure to the launch mounting erector cylinder and actuators for the umbilical mast, launching legs, fuel and oxidiser quick disconnect couplings, and the clamshells that secured the missile to the transporter/erector until the completion of fuelling operations (after which the transporter/erector would return to the horizontal under the damping influence of the erector cylinder ram). The unit could raise the Thor to the vertical firing position in something under a minute.

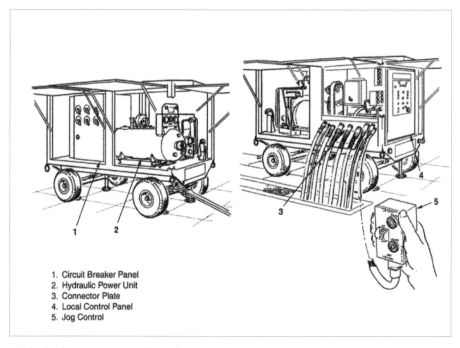

1. Circuit Breaker Panel
2. Hydraulic Power Unit
3. Connector Plate
4. Local Control Panel
5. Jog Control

The hydraulic pumping unit. (*USAF*)

Other essential components of the HPU were the electrical control units, which used 120V DC to operate the launch pin actuators and supplied electrical power to the launch mounting interlock switches (ensuring a set sequence of operations, such as shelter retraction before missile raising) and electrically controlled hydraulic equipment. Electrical, pneumatic, and hydraulic connectors were provided on the right-hand side of the HPU trailer.

Fuel

Possibly one of the most commonly documented facts about the missile is the type of fuel and oxidiser used by the engines. However, often the source of Thor's power is given very little further thought. In addition to describing how these propellants were stored and delivered to the waiting missile, this chapter sets out to examine these liquids, their properties, and production in a little more detail.

Thor's propulsion employed liquid fuels, which possess some distinct advantages over solid propellants. They are chemically more energetic, engines can be shut down, provide varying amounts of thrust (throttled), and even be restarted in flight, although the last two features noted here did not apply to Thor operations. A liquid fuel can also be routed to provide a measure of cooling (regenerative cooling) around the engine nozzle area before being burnt.

In addition to the fuel for the engines, missiles designed to leave the Earth's atmosphere must also carry an on-board oxygen supply (the oxidiser), without which the combustion process would not take place. There were a number of possible combinations of fuels and oxidisers available. Although all fuels, by the very nature of their intended application, can be deemed to be hazardous, some of these, especially in combination, were exceptionally dangerous, not just in terms of their volatility, but also in other risks involved to those charged with the responsibility for their storage and handling. Thor was fuelled by RP-1 and employed the cryogenic liquid oxygen (LOX) as an oxidiser.

A major disadvantage with liquid fuels, especially for a missile in a weapons application, is that the missile cannot be held fuelled with a cryogenic oxidiser for any great length of time. This impacts on the time required to prepare for launch and, ultimately, for a missile such as Thor (based in an above-ground location), its vulnerability in a situation where warning time of an incoming strike may be less than the time required to launch.

RP-1

The liquid fuel was produced from crude oil by means of the process of fractional distillation. This process is the separation of mixtures into their component parts, or fractions, an example of which is the separation of chemical compounds by their differing boiling points. Crude oil, heated and evaporated, is fed to a tall column (fractionating column) and the vapours allowed to condense at their respective temperatures. The column is very hot at the bottom, over 350° Celsius and progressively cools towards the top, in the region of 25° Celsius. Condensers are fitted at various heights in the column and substances that possess high boiling points, such as bitumen, which is used in road building, will remain at the bottom of the column as a residue. Substances that possess very low boiling points, an example of which would be bottled gas, as used for mobile cooking or heating, will condense out at the very top of the column. The intervening fractions, from bottom to top, would go through fuel oils, such as that used in power stations— diesel for cars and lorries, the kerosene fractions used in jet aircraft, naphtha used by the chemical industry. and gasoline (or petrol) for use in our cars. Each fraction will contain hydrocarbon molecules with a similar number of carbon atoms. The lower fractions have large molecules, a high boiling point, and are not very volatile. They do not flow readily and do not ignite easily. The top fractions, however, possess small molecules and a low boiling point. They are, by contrast, very volatile, flow readily, and ignite easily, all of which make the lighter fractions much more suitable for use as fuels.

Fuels of various types, some employing liquid oxygen (LO2 or LOX) as the oxidiser, had been previously investigated, but the degree of success was very variable. One such fuel tested was JP-4, an easily available wide-cut jet fuel, which is essentially a mixture, spanning the gasoline and kerosene boiling ranges (approximately 35° to 315° C (95°–600° F). JP-4, being kerosene cut with gasoline, possesses a higher volatility than normal kerosene fuels (approximate boiling range of 165°–290° C (330°–550° F)) and so presented a correspondingly greater difficulty in its handling, but a more immediate concern arose as Rocketdyne soon discovered that it deposited a heavy, tar-like residue in the engine cooling jackets and also soot and coke in the gas generators. JP-4 was therefore dismissed as a suitable fuel for rocket engines.

The solution to this issue would be a clean burn fuel and, with nothing immediately available from existing products, the oil industry was asked to develop a fuel with the required properties. A highly refined kerosene, which came to be known as RP-1, (rocket propellant no. 1), was therefore produced. This fuel, during production, was subjected to further treatments, such as acid washing and sulphur dioxide extraction. By doing this, substances that polymerise in storage (thus causing issues such as sludge in storage tanks and also affecting storage life of the fuel) were removed, as were sulphur-containing hydrocarbons. To meet the required specification, RP-1 could only be refined from crude oil with high naphthenic content and, at the time, the kerosene fractions suitable for its production were found only in the west-coast of the US. Although RP-1 still produced some residues in the engines, they were nothing like of the order previously seen. By the time that the ICBM and Thor programmes were established, it had become USAF policy to use RP-1 as the fuel and liquid oxygen as the rocket oxidiser.

RP-1 was covered by military specification MIL-R-25576.

Fuel Freezing Point: $-37.7°$ Celsius.

Flash Point: 43° Celsius.

Specific Gravity: 0.82.

Liquid Oxygen

Liquid oxygen, or LOX, the oxidiser used for Thor's engines, is obtained from air, also by means of the process of fractional distillation.

The air in our atmosphere consists of two main gases, nitrogen (about 78 per cent) and oxygen (about 21 per cent), both of which will liquefy at very low temperatures. To manufacture liquid oxygen, air is repeatedly compressed and cooled until a temperature below $-196°$ C, the boiling point of liquid nitrogen, is achieved. This, being colder than the $-183°$ C boiling point of liquid oxygen, results in a liquid that is a combination of both nitrogen and oxygen. To separate these components of the liquid, it is heated to a temperature higher than the boiling point of the liquid nitrogen, so that this component becomes gaseous again, but lower than the boiling point of the liquid oxygen at $-183°$ C, ensuring that the oxygen remains in liquid form.

Liquid oxygen is, when supplied, of 99.5 per cent purity. It is transparent, has no odour, and is a light blue in colour. As a possibly interesting aside, the paramagnetic properties of oxygen can be convincingly demonstrated with the use of LOX.

LOX was covered by military specification MIL-P-25508.

Freezing Point: $-219°$ Celsius.

Boiling Point: $-183°$ Celsius.

Specific Gravity: 1.145.

Liquid oxygen itself does not burn; however, it supports any combustion very vigorously. Although the liquid is generally stable, a mixture of liquid oxygen and a fuel is sensitive to shock. Any organic mixture in contact with liquid oxygen can spontaneously burn or detonate, although it is not usual for this to occur at ambient pressures. Should this combination suffer a sudden pressurisation, as it may in a propellant transfer to a missile, there is a much greater likelihood of this occurring.

As with most of Thor's development schedule, activities were taking place at the edge of technologies where there was no previous data or experience to which to refer or relate. Experience is, after all, largely a matter of things that we do and, fortunately, 'get away with'—any lessons learned forming a basis for future policies and decisions. Sometimes, we are not so lucky. One such tragic occasion was on 31 July 1958 at a Douglas facility at Sacramento, California. A valve and pressure regulator set up of a LOX storage tank end valve complex was being performed during a wet flow test. In the course of this test sequence, there was an explosion and fire.

A gaseous oxygen line suffered a failure and ruptured. Ignition occurred, which resulted in six men being seriously burned, three of whom—Oscar Udager, Walter J. Milan, and John May—later died from the injuries they received. Little was really known at that time about the handling of very large quantities of gaseous oxygen, and the terrible tragedy that occurred on this day highlights the daily dangers faced by those racing to establish Thor as an operational weapon system.

At this stage of development, the LOX storage tank was pressurised by gaseous oxygen, used to force the liquid oxygen along supply lines to the missile. Initially, the use of gaseous nitrogen had been considered for this purpose, but the designers of the system were concerned that gaseous nitrogen may be absorbed into the LOX and thus impair it as a propellant, with the attendant performance issues for Thor's engine. Accordingly, gaseous oxygen was employed.

Investigation of the accident concluded that the gaseous oxygen used to pressurise the LOX storage and supply system was vulnerable to contamination and this was the reason for the events of that day.

In order to avoid the recurrence of such an accident, gaseous nitrogen was once again examined as a potential pressurising gas for the LOX system. During testing, samples of LOX were taken at various stages of the propellant transfer procedure and were found to be uncontaminated by the nitrogen gas. Gaseous nitrogen was therefore adopted as the pressurising agent for the LOX storage and transfer system.

A short time after the accident at Sacremento, an engineer—Peter Portanova (later Dr Portanova)—working for the Douglas Aircraft Company, at Feltwell, moved on to the future 107 (SM) Squadron site at RAF Tuddenham as senior operations engineer. He was keen to emphasise the dangers of working with LOX to those in his charge. Along with a Douglas chemical process engineer, Ed White, he devised a practical demonstration. The demonstration involved a 1-foot diameter dish, a weight suspended from a string and pulley arrangement, a small amount of LOX, and the final and very important ingredient, his own thumbprint. The dish would be cleaned to laboratory standards and into its centre would be impressed the thumbprint. This small and seemingly insignificant action did in fact contaminate the otherwise scrupulously clean dish with hydrocarbon. With the addition of a small amount of LOX, carefully poured, the weight was released to drop directly onto the dish. The combination of the LOX and hydrocarbon, subjected to the shock of the arriving weight, was enough to cause an explosion that would, no doubt, have left a lasting impression on those who witnessed it.

A squadron commander, in conversation with the author, recalled an interesting event on a pad at his own site. As the LOX pit was being cleaned after having LOX discharged into it, a rare species of black rat, quite dead, was discovered. The remains were frozen and solid. It was thought that the rat and fallen into the pit and had avoided detection by climbing into the pipe from the missile. The danger here is that LOX in contact with anything organic, especially under pressure, as described above, always has the potential for instantaneous ignition. Fortunately, in this case, the incident passed safely; however, it did cause a few grey hairs. The LOX overflow pit, for this reason, had to be kept scrupulously clean, but, as it was open to the elements, this was much easier said than done.

Propellant Transfer System (PTS)

The propellant transfer system comprised the propellant storage tanks, pipeline equipment, skid mounted valve transfer units, and the associated equipment necessary for system monitoring and maintenance. There were two valve complexes for each tank. The no. 1 complex was at the missile end of the supply pipe trench, while the no. 2 complex was at the tank end. A metal shelter covered the valve complexes, which possessed both manual and automatic valves. Each automatic valve incorporated a manual bypass and there were purely manual valves for loading, draining, and venting. Propellant transfer to the missile was via the medium of gaseous nitrogen.

Storage

The fuel and oxidiser were stored in tanks on opposite sides of the launch emplacement. The RP-1 was to the left side of the pad centre line, looking from the rear of the emplacement, the LOX being to the right. The distance between the tank sites was in the region of 250 feet, ensuring that the propellants were kept well apart until they were transferred to the missile.

The RP-1 tank, the smaller of the two propellant storage tanks, had a capacity of approximately 6,500 US gallons (5,412 Imperial gallons/24,570 litres).

The amount of RP-1 to be loaded onto the missile for a launch would be calculated by the RP-1 computer that was located in a panel on the right-hand side of the electrical equipment trailer. The computer would be provided with the density of the fuel and the pressure in the fuel storage tank, and it based its calculations on this information. The fuel passed to the missile via a flow meter. The computer's calculations could be checked manually by means of a nomograph, a graphical device that would be entered with the relevant information and would provide a result that would agree, or otherwise, with the computer's output.

One issue that stored fuel can present is that of stratification. The fuel, if left, can stratify in the storage tank and this is based on the density of the constituent parts of the fuel, the fuel separating into layers, the heaviest components settling lower. Since the fuel feed line is near the bottom of the storage tank the heaviest components will get used first which may cause the density readings to be inaccurate. To combat issues such as this, the fuel tank was provided with a stratification pump, which would cause circulation in the tank and prevent the fuel from undergoing this process.

A check of the Propellant Transfer System (PTS) at RAF Driffield highlighted such an issue. The RP-1 computer output was checked by a nomograph calculation and this revealed that approximately 49 gallons of RP-1 had been under-loaded. Investigation of the issue concluded that an erroneous density reading had been fed to the computer as a result of the stratification pump having been turned off for the previous sixteen hours. The fuel storage tank pressure was also thought to have been high, which may have also caused an error in the computer pulse transmissions. The fuel was filtered by means of a mobile filter unit, which was located on the pad beside the RP-1 tank.

RP-1 was not loaded into the missile during a dual propellant flow exercise. In these conditions, the fuel supply pipe from the storage tank was connected to a flexible hose at the RP-1 Valve complex no. 1, the missile end of the supply pipe, and routed into a mobile tanker brought onto the pad for this purpose. The benefits of this were twofold. It did ensure safety in a scenario—however unlikely—that a sequence of events could lead to the accidental launch of a missile; however, it would appear that there were no facilities available in the UK for cleaning the RP-1 tank of any residues after a fuelling or de-fuelling process had been completed.

The atmospheric night photograph with the RP-1 tank nearest to the camera shows a wealth of detail. The background contains, from left to right, two nitrogen trailers, the smaller high-pressure nitrogen trolley, and the hydro-pneumatic distribution trailer, partially obscured by the blast wall. The RP-1 supply pipe was in a trench, supported by 'gallows units'. Unusually, the transporter/erector still has its rear road wheels attached.

The LOX storage tank, manufactured by the Cambridge Corporation of Lowell, Massachusetts, was at the time the largest air transportable storage container in the world. The reason that the LOX tank required such a large capacity was threefold. Firstly, because of the ratio of fuel to oxidiser burnt by the engines, the oxidiser tank on the missile was of much larger capacity than the fuel tank and it follows that a larger amount of LOX needed to be available. Secondly, as the LOX boils off when aboard the missile, the tank contents are depleting continuously, to the extent that in phase five (the last countdown phase before launch) the LOX tank needs to be finally topped up to capacity. Lastly, as a storage container was never going to be 100 per cent efficient, there was always a daily loss of the stored LOX.

The practical and transportable solution to maintaining the LOX in a liquefied state was to store it at very low temperature. To facilitate this, the tank was made in the form of a giant vacuum flask. It comprised two shells, the outer of which was made from aluminium in order to save weight, while the inner was constructed from precision-welded stainless steel sheet. The shells were of identical shape, separated by a gap in which a vacuum was maintained by a vacuum pump situated on the pad beside the LOX tank. Cylindrical in shape with hemispherical ends, the tank measured over 50 feet long by 8 feet high (15 × 2.5 metres), weighing some 32,000 lb (14,519 kg). The tank boasted a capacity of 13,500 US gallons (11,242 Imperial gallons or 51,039 litres). It was of monocoque construction, with rings around the circumference to provide some measure of stiffening. After manufacture, the interior of the inner shell was subjected to a specialised and rigorous cleaning process to ensure that the LOX would remain pure. The vacuum kept the rate at which heat could enter the LOX from the outside environment to a minimum. The average daily loss of LOX due to environmental issues was in the region of 40 to 50 gallons. On occasion, an ice-bridge would form between the inner and outer tanks and this physical bridging of the normally separated containers would constitute a quite serious issue, the loss of LOX increasing to a figure in the region of 150 gallons per day. A vacuum gauge, along with gauges to measure the liquid level and the vapour space pressure, was provided on the forward end of the tank.

The RAF contracted with the British Oxygen Company to keep the launch sites supplied with LOX, deliveries being required on a regular basis.

A Thor LOX tank found continued employment until the year 2000 with the RAF gas production flight, 217 Maintenance Unit at RAF Cardington, Bedfordshire.

The photograph of the LOX tank contains a great amount of other detail, which is worthy of note. It will be seen that the tank is contained in an open-ended enclosure, formed by low walls. At some sites, the LOX tank enclosure was in the form of a pit. This view also shows shelter and lighting gantry detail, with the number one nitrogen trailer nearest the camera and the number two trailer just

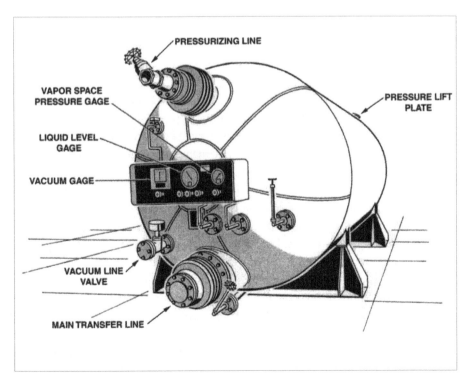

LOX tank detail. (*USAF*)

visible behind. The six technicians lend scale to the scene on this rather murky, and judging by their clothing, possibly cold day.

With the ever-present possibility of a technician at the launch emplacement coming into contact with LOX, white protective PVC over-suits were worn, giving an even greater science-fiction appearance to the scene during a countdown. The suit included a hood that incorporated a visor to protect the face and an apron to cover the shoulders, with rubber boots and elbow-length rubber gloves completing the ensemble for the well-dressed pad technician. On the LOX side of the pad, an emergency shower unit was provided for use in the event of contamination of personnel by the liquid. The shower would operate as soon as the cubicle door was opened.

The emergency shower cubicle appears nearest the camera in the photograph of the practice countdown. Immediately left of the cubicle is the LOX overflow basin. A technician wearing his protective suit is outlined against the mobile tanker used for dual-flow propellant exercises. Also of note is the transporter/erector back in the horizontal position and the ice surrounding the missile LOX tank.

The LOX supply pipe was routed through a U-shaped concrete channel, suspended at regular intervals by gallows units, on which were mounted spring-loaded canisters and turnbuckles. These devices were to allow for the uneven contraction in the stainless steel pipes as the LOX began to flow to the missile, causing the pipe to form into an arch.

Nitrogen

Fuel was fed to the missile by pressurising the storage tanks with gaseous nitrogen. The nitrogen was itself stored in four articulated trailers, the official nomenclature for which was compressed gas semi-trailers. There were two trailers located close to the LOX tank, on the up-range side of the launch emplacement, and the remaining two were positioned behind the blast wall on the opposite side of the emplacement. Each trailer carried 38 compressed gaseous nitrogen cylinders, charged to 3,500 psi. Pressure from the cylinders was fed into three manifolds, tapped at their centre by a main pipe, which led, via pressure gauges, to a main supply valve.

The nitrogen trailers located adjacent to the LOX tank were utilised to pressurise the liquid oxygen storage tank, purge and pre-pressurise the missile liquid oxygen tank, and supply purge pressure to the LOX transfer equipment when transfer operations were not in progress. Facing the control panel on the rear of the trailers, the No. 1 trailer was that on the left, while the No. 2 trailer was on the right.

The nitrogen trailers located behind the blast wall on the other side of the launch emplacement were utilised to pressurise the fuel storage tank, pre-pressurise the missile fuel tank, operate the pneumatic valves throughout the system, and for checkout and maintenance requirements. Facing the control panel on the rear of the trailers, the 'firing' nitrogen storage trailer was that on the left, while the 'checkout' nitrogen storage trailer was on the right. The supply from these trailers was routed directly into the trailer-mounted hydro-pneumatic systems controller (US nomenclature); this came to be known by the RAF as the nitrogen distribution trailer or, simply, the NDT. The NDT provided control and distribution of nitrogen for both the emplacement and the missile. It could handle pressures of up to 6,000 psi.

The interior of the nitrogen distribution trailer has been reported to the author as always possessing an odd smell. If inside, the door was left open as a safety precaution against the risk of being overcome due lack of oxygen.

MT drivers spent many hours on the road with nitrogen trailers, and one such driver recalled to the author his long journeys with these large trailers. The nitrogen cylinders were refilled at the British Oxygen Company's plant in Wolverhampton, the drivers delivering an empty trailer to the plant on one day and returning with a replenished trailer the next. The tractor unit employed for this task was usually a Leyland Hippo 10-ton chassis, in keeping with the UK policy to utilise British vehicles in connection with Thor operations for reasons of political sensitivity. However, the vehicle of choice, from the driver's point of view, was the American M-52, which had much lower geared and lighter steering and, with the front wheels well ahead of the driver, was much easier to handle. It was remembered, with some amusement, that manoeuvring the nitrogen trailers into the required position on the launch emplacement was a tricky process for several reasons, not the least of which was the 'helpful' and often conflicting advice offered by well-meaning bystanders—none of whom had actually driven an articulated lorry.

The small, trolley mounted high-pressure nitrogen storage tank, located next to the NDT, stored high-pressure nitrogen (6,000 psi) for pressurising the torus tanks in the missile warhead.

A necessary safety measure was that all equipment be electrically grounded. This prevented the buildup of a static charge, generated by the flow of RP-1 through the lines and also in passing from one storage container to another. A resultant spark discharge could have ignited any air or vapour mixture present. The launch emplacements themselves were fitted with a comprehensive earthing system.

EET, Missile Check-Out Trailer, and Power Switchboard

Electrical Equipment Trailer
Electrical equipment trailer (EET) was the RAF term for the trailer mounted launching countdown group. It was the major item of equipment on the emplacement and held all the critical equipment, such as guidance alignment set components, missile power supplies and battery charging, and warhead monitoring. Where appropriate, the panels are described in the relevant system text.

Missile Check-Out Trailer
The missile check-out trailer (MCOT) was only brought onto the launch emplacement as required. It was used to check equipment and provide simulation

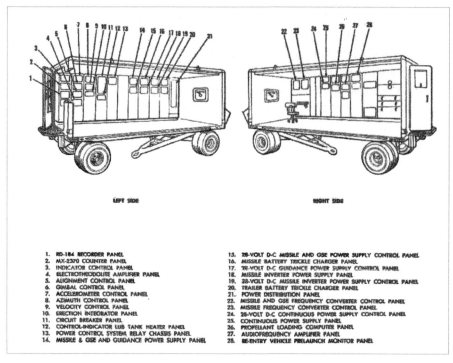

EET panel locations. (*USAF*)

of signals that it would not otherwise be possible to check routinely as part of the integrated system. For example, those during an actual launch. When not in use, the MCOT, at many sites, was parked on the launch control area. It is shown in place on the launch emplacement diagram.

Skid-Mounted Power Switchboard

The skid-mounted power switchboard was responsible for the distribution of power supplies to its respective launch emplacement. It received 480V 60-Hz AC power directly from the power distribution trailer located on the launch control area.

The switchboard contained three main elements. A 480V distribution panel, which distributed power to the emplacement equipment working at this voltage, while a second distribution panel supplied a 120–208V power supply, which was derived through the third element—a transformer.

Supplies at 480V and 120–208V were routed to the electrical equipment trailer, which possessed its own 120–208V distribution panel, while power supplies were made available at the emplacement position of the missile check-out trailer. The nitrogen distribution trailer and the missile shelter were provided with 120–208V distribution panels, 480V also being utilised for the shelter drive motor.

The EET provided a 28V DC power feed to the launch control trailer to power the continuous power bus bar for the consoles.

Guidance

The historical aspects of the guidance system and a detailed description of its airborne elements were included in the chapters covering the missile systems. This chapter describes the ground-based elements of the equipment.

With the exception of the guidance control panels, located in the launch control trailer, all other guidance equipment panels were situated in the electrical equipment trailer on the launch emplacement. The remaining elements of the system, the short-range and long-range theodolites, were mounted on the guidance platform near the nose of the missile and in a small building at the rear of the launch emplacement respectively.

The function of the ground-based equipment was to maintain the airborne guidance in a condition ready for use. It was also employed during the entry of target data into the missile's guidance computer and for pre-launch alignment of the missile's inertial guidance platform. Upon launch, the missile was autonomous and this equipment played no further role.

The preparation of the inertial guidance system for launch included the completion of two key operations. The stabilised platform within the airborne guidance had to be aligned so that its X axis (the down-range axis) was in alignment with the point at which the missile was aimed, the target azimuth. The airborne guidance set required the entry of the potentiometer settings, representing the velocity errors. The platform alignment and velocity error parameters to be set were the result of calculations made by a computer programme at the target planning stage. Of this, AC Spark Plug's Chief Engineer Thor Guidance, Paul O. Larson, recounting his time with Thor to the author in October of 2000, said:

> We created a trajectory model using an IBM 701 computer, a commercial scientific mainframe. While this seems mundane today, it was quite a challenge forty-five years ago. First, we created a model of a spherical, non-rotating Earth. Then we added the Earth's rotation. Then we changed the model from a spherical Earth to an oblate spheroid, larger at the equator than at the poles, as it really is. Then we built into the model the gravity anomalies that are significant to an inertial system. When all of this was done, we had a trajectory model that allowed targeting by inputting the latitude and longitude of the launch site and the latitude and longitude of the target. The model would then calculate the launch azimuth for the setting up of the theodolites and the potentiometer settings for the IGS analogue computer to be set into the guidance alignment console in the ground support equipment.

The data derived from the calculations determined the positioning of the theodolites and the series of numbers (the velocity errors) set into the guidance system. This data gave no hint of where the target might be. In stark contrast to the bomber crews who flew from these airfields not that many years before, and those who manned the contemporary V-force and Canberra squadrons surrounding the Thor launch sites, Thor launch crews received no briefing as to the location of their targets or why they were considered important enough to receive the attention of Thor's awesome payload. Some launch crew members did admit that this element made them feel a little uncomfortable, while one reported to the author that he and his colleagues spent many hours trying to guess the targets from the limited data they had. They knew the launch azimuth and, from knowledge of the flight time and the Earth's rotational speed, they could put together some crude numbers and examine maps to see if anything likely was in evidence, but whether any target was ever correctly guessed, they would never know.

The velocity errors were loaded into the guidance system on the ground and were, as in the case of the pitch and roll programme and the azimuth alignment of the stabilised platform, unique to the chosen target. Signals representing the errors could be sent to the airborne guidance set from the guidance control panel in the LCT or the velocity control in the EET. For setting, the clutches on the Vg potentiometers in the airborne guidance set were energised, causing them to respond to the operation of the counters for the X, Y, and Z channels on the ground equipment. When the counters were operated, transmitter synchros (a system whereby a generator (transmitter) and a motor (receiver) are connected by wiring, such that angular rotation or position in the transmitter is reproduced simultaneously in the receiver) sent signals to the receiver synchros for the corresponding channels in the airborne guidance set, which positioned the Vg potentiometer shafts to a specific point away from their 'zero reference' position. The signals were sent in the form of three groups of five numbers, one group for each of the X, Y, and Z channels. The settings were carefully monitored and, to that end, were checked several times a day. A launch crew coming on duty and the crew going off duty would check the settings together before the on-coming crew accepted responsibility for the systems about to pass into their care. At other times during the day, the squadron commander would make no-notice inspections to verify the correct data entry. If a target change was ordered—for example, from target one to target two—the Vg potentiometers would have to be adjusted to their 'on zero' positions and then reset to reflect their new positions. A squadron commander, in conversation with the author, reported that, on average, the time to achieve this was in the region of four minutes.

The guidance system was not kept in a permanent state of launch readiness. Had it been so, launch countdown times could have been reduced, but at the expense of extra wear and tear on the equipment, especially the all-important gyros, with the attendant issues of increased maintenance, cost and reliability concerns. One feature of the guidance system, however, was permanently operating. This was the gyro heating. The gimbal and gyro assemblies of the gyroscopes were floated in a very dense fluid, about twice the density of water, the fluid temperature having to be very strictly controlled in order to achieve a constant gimbal gain and, consequently, consistent system performance. The gyro heaters were monitored at the continuous status section of the launch control console operator's missile monitor panel in the LCT and at the theodolite amplifier panel in the EET. The crews came to call the practice of monitoring the gyro heating as bird watching, 'bird' being the American slang term for the missile. Although the continuous alignment concept had been considered, Thor's guidance system remained in a relaxed state and was brought up to operational readiness when required during phase one (the electrical phase) of the launch countdown, when the guidance system proceeded through its own countdown to become fully aligned.

There were seven possible modes of the guidance system: off, standby, power on, align step one, align step two, align step three, and complete.

A simple *précis* of the major guidance countdown events appears below, and a full listing of the actions that occurred during an automatic guidance countdown is presented at the end of this chapter.

At 'off', in addition to gyro heating, there was distribution of 28V DC main power.

'Standby' was the mode in which the guidance equipment would normally be held, unless a launch countdown or maintenance was in progress. While in this mode, GSE 115V single-phase 60-Hz AC and IGE 115V three-phase 400-Hz AC power was available to the associated equipment.

At 'power on', there was distribution of 28V DC to the airborne guidance set, with 270V DC and 115V 400-Hz three-phase AC being supplied to the GSE. Stabilisation gyros and gimbals were prepared for alignment.

Thor made extensive use of synchro systems, but, as these could only produce a small torque, a requirement to move something of a reasonable mass required another solution; usually, a device known as an amplidyne was employed. An amplidyne (now obsolete) was an electromechanical amplifier and utilised a special type of motor-generator (usually an AC motor driving a DC generator). It used the technique of regeneration to increase its gain, and in certain forms, it was capable of moving a very large mass. At this stage, Thor's on-board amplidyne (PU-424), used for the gimbal torque motors, was started and monitored, as was the guidance generator (PU-411), a motor-generator (M-G) set used for the conversion of the frequency, voltage or phase of the input power, as may be required for its associated equipment.

During the next steps of the guidance countdown, the align steps, the guidance system alignment became increasingly accurate, while the maintenance of that alignment was gradually transferred to the on-board equipment.

The gyros reached their operating speed. There followed a period in which the stabilised platform gimbal system achieved a coarse alignment. During this time, the vertical sensing element (VSE) output maintained the alignment of the pitch and roll axes (missile horizontal). The pitch and roll null meters would register the output of the VSE, while the yaw axis null meter would register the output of the short-range theodolite. The VSE, which can simply be thought of as an electronic form of spirit level, was a function of the flight control system high-*g* gyros. Once aligned, the platform stabilisation gyros took over the task of maintaining platform alignment. Introducing the stabilisation gyros also caused some issues brought about by small imperfections in the gyros themselves and the fact that the Earth is rotating. The necessary corrections for these errors were provided by the erection control in the alignment set components. The stabilisation torque amplifier circuitry maintained the alignment of the stabilised platform by using the outputs of the stabilisation gyros and the earth rate and gyro unbalance correction signals, correcting the effects of the Earth's rotation and any gyro unbalance. While the missile is awaiting launch, the stabilised platform gyros suffered wander. Wander is defined as the movement of the spin axis of the gyroscope away from the reference frame in which it is set. There are two types of wander, real and apparent. Real wander occurs where manufacturing imperfections, such as friction or unbalance, in the gyro cause the spin axis to physically move, hence the term real wander. It was to minimise this effect that so much intensity of labour was expended on the gyros during the manufacturing process. Despite these efforts, there remained a need for Thor's guidance alignment set to provide gyro unbalance signals to counter these built-in inaccuracies. Apparent wander is due to the Earth's rotation. The single-degree-of-freedom gyroscope, such as those used to stabilise Thor's platform, is, fortunately, the easiest to consider as it has only one input and one output axis. A gyroscope defines its direction with reference to inertial space, and to remain referenced to any direction on the Earth's surface, it must be corrected for apparent wander. A gyro at a point on the Earth's surface is affected according to the alignment of its input axis. If the input axis were aligned with the Earth's spin axis, earth rate—that is, the rate of rotation of the Earth (15.04 degrees per hour)— would be detected. If the input axis should be aligned with the local vertical, the gyro would be said to be suffering drift, and it would drift at the rate of 15.04 × sine of its latitude (degrees per hour). Should the input axis be orientated to local north, the gyro would be said to be toppling at a rate of 15.04 × cosine of its latitude (degrees per hour). Finally, with the input axis aligned with local east—that is, at right angles to the Earth's rotational vector—it would not detect any component of Earth rotation. The reader should refer to the erection control diagram (see p. 157) and the full countdown for the technique used to counter the errors.

At the end of the guidance countdown sequence, the system passed into complete mode. The platform stabilisation gyros were maintaining the platform alignment and the voltages cancelling the effect of the Earth's rotation were now held at a constant value. A relay operated to forward a signal notifying 'guidance aligned'. The operation of this relay, along with others of the missile's major systems, was required in order to signal the completion of phase one of the launch countdown. The guidance countdown is reproduced at the end of this chapter, along with diagrams of the alignment set components and a brief description of their function.

Short-Range Theodolite

During the guidance countdown, an integral part of phase one of the launch countdown, the X (down-range) axis of the stabilised platform had to be aligned with the aiming point of the missile. While the missile was in the horizontal position, it was the function of the short-range theodolite (SRT) to provide the necessary azimuth reference for accurate platform alignment.

Every Thor was equipped with a choice of two targets, and as the aiming point for each would be different, azimuth alignment for either target was made possible by the provision of two short-range theodolites, designated Target 1 SRT and Target 2 SRT. The theodolites were mounted on a structure running parallel to the launch emplacement centreline, near to the nose of the missile and termed the guidance platform (not to be confused with the stabilised platform). The position of the guidance platform was highly accurately surveyed, and a brass stud set into the concrete marked the centre of the structure. An opening provided on the right-hand side of the missile airframe allowed the SRT to gain optical access to the guidance system.

The SRT comprised two main elements, a lower portion, the monitoring optical system, and the upper portion, the visual optical system. Manufactured by Perkin-Elmer of Norwalk, Connecticut, it contained the components and circuitry necessary to maintain the stabilised platform in alignment. The visual optical system was a modified precision surveyor's transit telescope, manufactured by Keuffel and Esser of Hoboken, New Jersey, the function of which was to ensure that the SRT was correctly positioned. The operation of both elements is described later in the text.

The two elements of the SRT were mated on a common vertical axis, about which they were free to rotate independently; they could also be locked together and the complete unit could be locked to the guidance platform rail on which they were mounted.

Within the monitoring optical system was an illuminated scale, viewed via a microscope eyepiece, graduated in degrees, minutes, and seconds, indicating the angular difference in azimuth between the monitoring and visual optical systems. In operation, the angle set between the two systems was a key element of stabilised platform alignment, and to assist in the fine adjustment of the precise settings required, vernier and micrometre type adjustment facilities were provided. It was essential that the theodolite was absolutely level when in operation and a bubble level and levelling screws were provided.

The drawing of the short-range theodolite shows the right-hand side of the instrument. The left-hand side features a Hobbs-type meter, indicating the number of hours for which the instrument was powered.

The SRT was an azimuth alignment theodolite, the basic principle of which was to transmit a beam of light to an object, a reflective surface mounted on which directed the light beam back to an integral monitoring system. When in alignment, the reflective surface was perpendicular to the light beams transmitted by the theodolite. Any error in alignment would cause the light beams to be reflected at an angle equal to the angle (in relation to the normal, a line perpendicular to the mirror surface) at which the light beams struck the mirror surface.

The reflected light beams therefore provided information as to whether there was any error in alignment between the object and the pre-determined position of the theodolite. The theodolite circuitry was arranged such that the direction of an error could be determined. This information was used by the alignment set components to drive the object, in this case, the yaw gimbal of the inertial guidance system, back into alignment with the theodolite.

The theodolite control circuit was one function of the theodolite amplifier panel in the alignment set components and switched one of the two SRTs into the azimuth alignment loop. The SRT selected was dependent upon the position of the target one and target two switch at the target selection panel on the launch control console operator's upper panel. The target could also be set in the EET at the alignment control panel (see alignment set component diagram, p. 149).

There were two amplifier channels, which for simplicity will be referred to as channel one and channel two. Only one channel was utilised for an individual target, the output from channel one being used for target one and that from channel two for target two.

Two glow tubes were provided with 270V DC by the relevant amplifier channel, and they were modulated at a frequency of 400 Hz. The modulators in the amplifier channels impressed a pulsating signal upon the 270V DC voltage feeding the glow tubes, the inputs to which were 180 degrees out of phase so that the glow tubes illuminated alternately.

Two light beams were therefore generated and these passed through a collimating lens and were transmitted to the reflecting optics on the yaw gimbal of the stabilised platform and reflected back to the theodolite.

The theodolite incorporated a truncated prism, this having an aperture in the form of a slit at its front edge, behind which was positioned a photo-multiplier light-sensitive tube. When light flux fell onto the tube, a signal would be generated. If the monitored reflector on the yaw gimbal was perpendicular to the light beams from the theodolite, and therefore in alignment, then the two beams returned at positions equally distant from the central axis of the optical system and very little flux passed through the slit aperture at the tip of the prism. Any flux passing through the slit in this case would also contain both signals, out of phase by 180 degrees, thereby cancelling each other out. This condition is known as a true null. Should the reflecting surface not be perpendicular to the transmitted beams (and therefore not aligned with the theodolite), then one of the return beams would

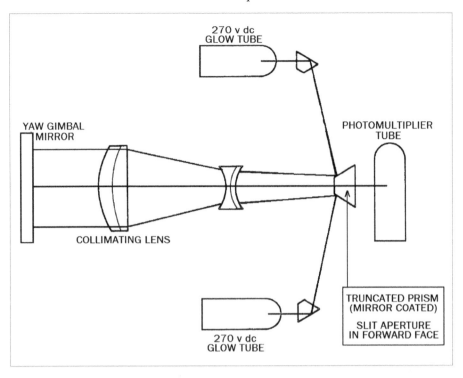

Simplified schematic diagram of a SRT monitoring optical system. (*Author's Collection*)

move into the slit and the flux received by the photo multiplier tube served as an error signal. Sensing the phase of the 400-Hz error signal allowed identification of the beam within the slit and hence the determination of the direction of the error. Within the amplifier channel, the error signal was filtered, amplified, and then routed to the guidance set to drive the yaw gimbal back into alignment.

There could, however, exist a condition where the monitored gimbal was so far out of alignment that neither of the reflected light beams would enter the slit, causing no error to be detected by the photo-multiplier tube. This condition is known as a false null. To avert this possibility, both light sources in the theodolite were modulated with a second frequency of 800 Hz and in phase coincidence. Therefore, during a condition of a true null, when small amounts of light flux from both beams entered the slit, the 800-Hz signal would also be present. In the false null condition, this signal would clearly be absent. The output of the photo multiplier tube detected that the 800-Hz signal was not present, thereby indicating that the light beams were not being received back by the theodolite. The lack of the 800-Hz signal could be employed to cause the gimbal to hunt until the signal is detected, at which time the theodolite would resume normal operation.

The output of the error signal filters was also fed to a theodolite acquired light circuit. The signal in the circuit was amplified and applied to a switching circuit, which operated when an azimuth alignment error signal was not applied to the amplifier channel; in other words, a true null condition existed, causing the illumination of the 'THEODOLITE ACQUIRED' lamp on the back of the SRT. If an azimuth error signal was present, a relay in the switching circuit was de-energised, which illuminated the 'SIGNAL' lamp on the back of the SRT.

Stabilised Platform Alignment

During the description of the SRT, it was shown that the stabilised platform was correctly aligned when the mirror on the yaw gimbal was in a plane perpendicular to the line of sight of the theodolite. The yaw gimbal was the outermost gimbal of the system and was orientated in line with the longitudinal axis of the missile. With the missile in the horizontal position, the yaw gimbal axis was in a vertical plane, which would allow the gimbal to be rotated in order to position the entire gimbal system such that the X axis of the stabilised platform was in alignment with the aiming point of the missile (the diagram in the airborne guidance section refers).

Although launch emplacements were constructed with their centrelines set to a predetermined direction with respect to true north, allowing a launch in only this direction would be severely limiting. Therefore, a choice of targets from any given emplacement was afforded by allowing the selection of targets whose aiming point lay within an arc of 15 degrees to each side of the centreline direction. The difference in direction between the target azimuth and the emplacement centreline was accounted for by the provision of a roll programme within the missile flight control system and by pre-launch SRT alignment of the stabilised platform. Therefore, it follows that the SRT must be set at an angle appropriate to the required target azimuth in order for the yaw gimbal mirror to be perpendicular to the SRT light beams when the system is correctly aligned. It will also be seen that the direction in which the theodolite transmitted its beams of light was at precisely 90 degrees to the target azimuth

Taking the case of a target azimuth along the launch emplacement centreline, the guidance system was correctly aligned when the yaw gimbal, and hence the X axis of the stabilised platform, were in exact alignment with the centreline of the launch emplacement. From the discussion of SRT positioning, it follows that the light beams emitted by the optical monitoring unit would be at precisely 90 degrees to this direction. The centre point of the guidance platform was the datum point, or benchmark, for this launch azimuth, and this is where the SRT would be positioned.

For any other target azimuth, the SRT would need to be set to the appropriate angle relative to the launch emplacement axis, so that when the perpendicular relationship of the yaw gimbal mirror to the SRT light beams was established, the X axis of the stabilised platform was aligned with the aiming point of the missile.

The launch azimuth was known, and without any physical constraints posed by such issues as mirror size and optical access to the airframe, the SRT could simply be rotated to the required angle. The above issues did, however, preclude this simple adjustment. For the theodolite to maintain optical contact with the yaw gimbal mirror, the additional measure of physically moving the SRT along the guidance platform rail became necessary. The distance and direction of SRT movement was a function of the required azimuth.

For a target azimuth to the left of the launch emplacement centreline (looking down-range), the SRT would need to aim its light beams to the left of a line perpendicular to the guidance platform rail. The yaw gimbal would therefore be required to rotate to the left, anti-clockwise, to align the stabilised platform with the launch azimuth. However, it should be remembered that to maintain optical contact, the SRT must be physically moved—in this case, down-range, or towards the front end of the launch emplacement.

The distance that the SRT would need to be moved along the rail can be illustrated by the application of some simple trigonometry. This distance was a function of the tangent of the change of angle in azimuth. The distance from the guidance platform rail to the reflecting surface on the yaw gimbal was 127 inches; therefore, for a change in azimuth of 1 degree, the distance of SRT movement would be $\tan(1) \times 127 = 2.217$ inches. It therefore follows that for the full 15 degrees change in azimuth, the distance would be some 34.03 inches ($\tan(15) \times 127$), which accounts for the length of the guidance platform rail. The technique used for the precise positioning of the SRT along the rail will be discussed later. In this example, after launch the pre-programmed flight profile would command the missile to roll to the left, bringing the missile yaw axis in a vertical plane through the cut-off trajectory. A target azimuth to the right of the launch emplacement centre line would require the reverse of the above, the SRT movement being up-range or towards the rear of the launch emplacement. After launch, the pre-programmed flight profile would now command the missile to roll to the right.

The setting of the precise angle of the SRT in relation to the guidance platform and hence launch emplacement axis was a function of the visual optical system, the upper element of the SRT. An angle, calculated from previously known data entered into a simple formula, was set between the monitoring optical system and the visual optical system. This was achieved through the illuminated scale in the monitoring optical system, viewed through the microscope eyepiece. The angle, in degrees, minutes, and seconds, was set according to the calculations, and the upper and lower elements of the SRT were locked together. The complete SRT could still be rotated on its axis, and by rotating the entire assembly until the visual optical system was aligned with the emplacement guidance platform axis, the process was completed. The requirement for absolute accuracy cannot be over emphasised and the effort expended in manufacturing the system to such fine tolerances would be to no avail if it were all to be let down by imprecise alignment of the SRT with the platform axis. It is clear that an extremely accurate method of achieving this last stage of SRT alignment was required and this came in the form of the collimator.

Collimator

At both ends of the guidance platform was a substantial post, each supporting a collimator, one for each SRT. The collimator, an optical instrument, provided the means for precise alignment of the SRT in relation to the guidance platform axis. Collimated light is, simply, light rays that are parallel and will disperse minimally with increasing distance—often said to be focused at infinity. The collimator projected a beam of collimated green light, which contained an illuminated reticule (a network of fine lines, in this case two perpendicular cross-hairs in the form of an 'X') that was set exactly at the focal length of the objective lens. The projected, collimated reticule target provided a reference line of sight, against which the optical monitoring system telescope, also provided with a cross-hair reference, would be precisely aligned. This ensured that the SRT, locked to the optical system at the required angle, would bring the X axis of the stabilised platform to alignment with the target azimuth with equal precision. The complete SRT would then be locked to the guidance platform rail. With the optical telescope and the collimator in alignment, accuracy was stated to be within one arc second.

The collimator, manufactured by Davidson Optronics, Inc., was a substantial instrument, its basic measurements being some 11 inches long × 7 inches wide × 7 inches high (27.9 × 17.8 × 17.8 cm). It weighed in at a surprising 34.6 lb (15.7 kg). The objective lens was of 2.5 inches (6.35 cm) diameter.

Target Reference Pillar

Each launch site was provided with target reference pillars. These structures were some 13 feet high and were constructed from concrete tubing filled with reinforced concrete. Most sites seem to have been provided with three pillars, although some sites did have more—notably 240 Squadron at Breighton and 150 Squadron at Carnaby, boasting four each.

The pillars were sited in during the initial surveys of the launch site by reference to the pole star, Polaris, and provided a known reference point in relation to true north for the particular launch pads that each pillar served. The position of the pillars and their pairing with the pads that would use them were clearly marked on the Air Ministry Works Directorate site plans. In providing this permanent, known reference, the need to sight Polaris again was avoided. To ensure guidance accuracy, it was absolutely vital that the pillars remained vertical, this accounting for the very substantial nature of their construction and the regular surveys conducted by visiting teams of Royal Engineers. Half a century after the Thor sites were abandoned, often the only tell-tale sign of the location of a site as one passed by was the vision of a target pillar still standing stiffly to attention over the bleak landscape, which mostly concealed the other remains.

The pillars were used in the setting up and the regular checking of the theodolites, to ensure that the correct launch azimuth was being maintained. The pillar was topped by a flat metal plate, upon which was mounted four locating bolts or studs. When a theodolite was to be set up or the target angles checked, a similar metal plate, into which four holes were drilled, was placed on top of the pillar and located on the studs. In the centre of the plate, and now held firmly on the vertical axis of the pillar, was a vertical metal rod, approximately 9 inches in height and of half an inch diameter (22.9 × 1.3cm). This was the actual target to be sighted by the visual optical system telescope mounted on the theodolite. The angle from the theodolite to the target reference pillar for a particular target was a known value. This angle would be set, using the illuminated scale in the monitoring optical system, viewed through the microscope eyepiece. The vertical cross-hair reticule in the visual optical system would then coincide with the centre of the target rod when the theodolite was precisely positioned on its rail. The metal rod is, clearly, a very small target, especially when consideration is given to the fact that the pillar was often over 800 feet away from the pad that it served. In this way, the theodolite could be set up and checked, the accuracy achieved generally intended to be within one arc second.

Long-Range Theodolite

It was the purpose of the long-range theodolite (LRT) to maintain stabilised platform alignment subsequent to the missile being raised to the vertical and as a result, losing contact with the short-range theodolite (SRT).

There were some marked contrasts between the operating environment of the LRT and the SRT. Whereas a separate SRT was provided for each target, there was only one LRT for each missile. Clearly, the LRT would need to be capable of monitoring the alignment of the stabilised platform for both targets. While the SRT was maintaining alignment, the missile was held securely by its transporter-erector in a horizontal position just over 10 feet away. During LRT alignment, however, the missile, now vertical, was subject to external factors, notably wind and the fuelling process, both of which would cause the missile to sway on its launch mounting. Therefore, the LRT had to maintain accurate alignment of the stabilised platform, despite the sway or translation of the missile, from a distance of 425 feet.

It will be recalled that, with the missile horizontal, the yaw gimbal, monitored by the SRT, maintained the azimuth alignment of the stabilised platform. With the missile in the vertical position, however, the geometry of the gimbal system precluded this and, consequently, the stabilised platform azimuth alignment became a function of the roll gimbal, monitored by the LRT.

Due to the operating environment of the LRT, the simultaneous monitoring of two reflective elements would be required. The chosen elements required particular properties, which would provide a ready means to distinguish between a deviation in azimuth of the stabilised platform (rotation) and the sway of the missile airframe itself (translation). The LRT was required to sense these deviations, determine their direction and magnitude, and provide signals that would result in a corrective response appropriate to the condition detected.

The fundamental principles of the LRT remain basically similar to those of the SRT; a light source was transmitted to reflective elements at the missile and was received back at the theodolite. The theodolite responded as required in order to maintain the received coded light signals in balance, or nulled, hence maintaining the alignment of the stabilised platform. The issues of distance and sway, however, required a very different approach to its design. This theodolite consisted of three separate assemblies. The first assembly was in a fixed position, while the other two assemblies—a constant deviation reflector, in the form of a penta prism, and a receiver to detect the rotation of the stabilised platform—were mounted on a movable base, the freedom of movement of which was in the lateral sense—that is, perpendicular to the line of sight to the missile.

The fixed assembly contained the light source. The LRT operated on only one source of light, which, because of the distance involved, needed to be very powerful and would almost certainly have been in the form of an arc lamp, now termed a gas discharge lamp. Several sources reported to the author that the light emitted was an intense white/blue light, which would tend to suggest that the source used xenon. The other elements of the fixed assembly were, in order from the light source, a re-imaging lens, a source slit, choppers for coding the light source, and a source lens. The source lens was divided into two halves, left and right, which will be discussed later. The fixed assembly also contained the receiver that would the detect missile sway or translation. This unit was required to be set in line with the light source and was situated in the gap between the two halves of the source lens, possessing its own lens to focus the returning light upon the receiver.

Operation

A lens was situated in front of the light source to re-image the light source at a point known as a source slit. The slit was required due to the inevitable missile translation. It was essentially because the receiver for the rotational (azimuth) information was not in a fixed position relative to the prism that reflected its information once missile translation was taken into account; this affected the accuracy of the rotational measurement. Without the translation, the reflector edges would naturally provide the horizontal limits of the system and the slit would not be required. Translation of the missile, however, would almost certainly ensure that the reflector and receiver combination would pass outside the limits for the required level of accuracy. The inclusion of the slit provided a method whereby the horizontal limits of the light beam, at the reflector, could be suitably restricted so as to provide an apparent 'fixed' relative position for the reflector and the receiver while the missile was translating. Subject to the proviso that the entire width of the restricted beam remained within the reflector, accurate measurement of the rotation of the reflector about its vertical axis could be assured. The above is not, however, a panacea for all issues of translation; depending upon the magnitude of the translation, the provision of the slit may not be enough. The result of this was that an additional solution to the issue of translation had to be found and this will be described later.

Having passed through the source slit, the light went on to the coding process. As the LRT operated on a single light source, the coding was achieved by use of a device known as a chopper. Choppers, which come in various forms, simply interrupt the light beam and allow light to pass for a certain, known period. Perhaps a form of chopper with which we are all familiar will be the signal lamp seen in movies, used for signalling between aircraft or ships. The lamp is continuously illuminated in the signal light and the operator simply modulates a shutter device to allow light to pass for a defined period, usually to code the light into dots and dashes of a known relationship in order to produce an output in the form of Morse code. The coding of the light source in the LRT was similar in principle, but with the use of highly sophisticated techniques.

The choppers would interrupt the light beam such that light would be allowed to pass through the source lens, which was itself divided by a central gap, first through one side and then the other, on a continuously alternating 'left–right' basis. The chopping was very precisely controlled, being at a constant, known frequency and having a precisely determined phase relationship to a reference voltage. This would essentially give the beam from each side of the source lens its own identity.

Having passed through the source lens, the now coded light travelled to the constant deviation optical device, a penta prism. A penta prism is a five-sided reflecting prism that is used to deviate a beam of light by a constant 90 degrees, even though the entry beam itself may not have been at exactly 90 degrees to the prism. The beam reflects inside the prism twice, allowing the transmission of an image through a right angle without inverting or reversing it. This means that the image is transmitted onward without changing its 'handedness' as would an ordinary prism or mirror. This device transmitted the coded light energy to both of the reflective elements, but due to the properties of those elements, only received reflected energy from the element for missile translation. The reflected light from the rotational sensing element went directly to its own detector.

The two reflective elements, possessing very different properties, were provided to ensure that the LRT could accurately monitor the stabilised platform despite missile translation.

The first was an element that would be sensitive to changes of the angle of the incident light and would cause the angle of the light reflected to vary accordingly; however, the information provided by this reflective element was restricted to the variation in angle about a single axis, in this case the vertical, so that the variations measured would be in rotation or azimuth. In order to function correctly, this element would need to be equally insensitive to any changes in the incident light about a second axis, which was perpendicular to the rotational axis. This is the axis along which the missile sway would be measured. Conversely, the second element would need to be insensitive to changes in light caused by rotation about the vertical axis, but sensitive to changes about the 'sway' axis. In actuality, rather than a reflective element, such as a mirror or a prism, a retroflector (or retro-reflector) could be employed in this role because it would be insensitive to any changes in incident light.

The reflector for the rotational element of the monitoring system was a 'roof' prism. It is so named as it resembles the shape of a basic house roof, sloping sides meeting at an apex. The prism was mounted with the apex running horizontally and furthest away from the light source. It was actually a porro prism, named after its inventor Ignazio Porro and is basically one corner of a glass cube in the form described, with right-angled triangular end faces completing the 'house roof'. When a light source falls on the prism, it enters at the rectangular face, is reflected twice internally from the sloping roof faces, and exits, again via the rectangular face. Due to the way the light enters and exits the prism, at normal incidence, it does not split the light into its component colours. An image entering the prism is rotated by 180 degrees and exits in the opposite direction, offset from its entrance point. A very important feature is that, due to the image being reflected twice, the 'handedness' of the image is unchanged.

The sway element of the monitoring system was a retroflector, which is designed to reflect light back to its source with the minimum of scattering. The light is reflected back to the source parallel to the incoming light, but opposite in direction. An ordinary mirror system could only do this if it were exactly perpendicular to the source of incoming light. The retroflector had three equal sectors of 120 degrees and was slightly cone-shaped, with an apex at the centre and furthest from the light source. Excellent everyday examples of retroflective surfaces are the 'battenberg' squares on the sides of emergency vehicles and the markings on high-visibility clothing. It would also be possible to utilise another porro prism, subject to certain provisos, set at 90 degrees to the first prism.

Rotation

The reflective elements were arranged vertically, the porro prism being the lower of the two. It was very important that the light source illuminated the entire vertical extent of the prism so that the only changes in the angle of the reflected light would be those that were caused by the changes in the incident light in the horizontal plane—that is, due to rotation.

Light from the source was transmitted via the penta prism to the porro prism on the roll gimbal of the stabilised platform. The reflected light energy was returned to the theodolite, collected by a lens system, and passed through an aperture into the rotation detector. If the stabilised platform went out of alignment, the detector unit would not be receiving equal amounts of the light energy from the two coded parts of the light beam. This would cause the detector to generate an output signal indicating the unbalance. The signal was compared to a reference signal that had a known time and phase relationship to the light coding process. The result of the comparison indicated, by its amplitude, the amount of rotational deviation of the stabilised platform and, by its phase, the direction in which the platform had moved.

The error signals generated were routed through the alignment set components to the torque motor on the roll gimbal, driving the stabilised platform back into alignment. Once aligned, the rotational detector would be receiving equal amounts of light energy and the null condition restored.

The LRT projected its light beam directly to the missile from the rear of the launch emplacement, the line taken having been the subject of a first order survey, and is in the same direction for both targets. As the azimuth for each target would be different, a method was required for making an allowance for these variations. It was seen that, for the SRT, the target azimuth was accounted for by positioning the theodolite along a rail, the distance illustrated as being a function of the tangent of the angle between the launch emplacement centreline and the offset in azimuth for the particular target. This, clearly, would not be an option in this case as the rail length would need to be some 228 feet. Fortunately, a relatively simple solution was to hand, and the issue of variation in target azimuth was overcome by the setting of the porro prism to the relevant angle. In aligning the gimbal so that the coded light signals were nulled, it will be appreciated that a difference in 'mirror angle' will result in a different stabilised platform azimuth, even though the incoming light arrives from the same angle for both targets.

Translation

A method of determining and allowing for the translation of the missile was required because the sway of the missile, causing a change in the relative position of the porro prism, would be wrongly perceived as a change in azimuth of the stabilised platform by the rotation detector. This is due to the limitations of maintaining the light beam within the confines of the porro prism as described earlier, and would result in the issue of an erroneous correction, which would, in turn, cause a real error in azimuth alignment. The answer to this problem was simply to move the rotation detector in sympathy with the missile translation in order to maintain its relationship with the porro prism.

The major component of this solution to the issues of translation was the penta prism, which was employed for the property of deviating a beam of light by a constant 90 degrees, even though the entry beam itself may not have been at exactly 90 degrees to the prism. If the penta prism had not been placed in the system, the light source itself would have needed to move in order to maintain the null signal when the missile was translating. Even slight variations in alignment of the light source could have resulted in overall large erroneous errors in the degree of translation detected.

This potential error was avoided by having the light source remain in a fixed position and to arrange for the penta prism to also be moved in sympathy with the missile translation, thereby maintaining the null condition. This solution provided an additional advantage. The light source would be transmitted to the reflective elements on the missile at the same angle, even if the light beam itself did not enter the penta at exactly 90 degrees. Therefore, any minor variations in the alignment of the base to which the penta and the rotation detector were fixed, for instance due to mechanical play in the actuators, would be automatically corrected.

The reflective element for the detection of missile sway was a retroflector. The desirable property of this was that it would reflect a light beam back parallel to the path that it travelled to reach the retroflector, despite the fact that there may be some considerable change in the angle of incidence of the light.

The coded light beam, via the retroflector, travelled back parallel to, but opposite in direction to its original path. Once again, it entered the penta prism. It was now retransmitted through the penta and, in travelling back towards the source from which it came, was directed via a lens to the sway detector unit that was positioned directly in line with the light source, between the two halves of the source lens.

If the light source slit image was positioned centrally in the apex of the retroflector, the sway detector unit would receive equal quantities of light energy from each part of the returned coded light beam and a balanced condition, or null, would exist. If there should be any lateral translation of the missile, however, the retroflector would not be illuminated symmetrically. As a result, the sway detector unit would detect a greater amount of coded light energy originating from one half of the source lens and a correspondingly lesser amount originating from the other. This would cause the detector to generate an output signal indicating the unbalance. The signal was compared to a reference signal that had a known time and phase relationship to the light coding process. The result of the comparison indicated, by its amplitude, the amount of missile lateral translation and, by its phase, or sense, the direction in which the missile had moved.

It was so arranged that the output of the error signal from the sway detector would be amplified in a servo-amplifier and fed onward to drive a servo-mechanism, which would cause the base, upon which the penta and the rotational detector were affixed, to be driven in the appropriate direction. When the light source beam transmitted by the penta 'caught up' with the retroflector once again, symmetry of the coded parts of the reflected light and, hence, the null condition would be restored and movement of the base would cease.

It should be remembered that the coded light energy received by the rotation detector was reflected by the porro prism, which, as configured for this application, was insensitive to changes in incident light in the vertical plane. The result of this was that the movement of this detector due to lateral movement of the penta prism did not affect the normal operation of the rotational detector unit.

The LRT was prepared for use at the outset of a countdown. The initial instruction was to start generators (those on the LCA) and switch on the long-range theodolite. The moveable element of the LRT would be set to its datum mark and the elevation and azimuth settings checked. According to an entry in the ORB (Form 540) for 106 (SM) Squadron at Bardney, the average time to capture the LRT was approximately thirteen seconds. In the event that the LRT became unavailable, there was a facility for referencing the roll gimbal to the airframe. This was via the airframe azimuth reference loop. This loop was activated by pressing the 'airframe az. ref.' switch. The integral lamp would light to indicate that the loop was active. Upon pressing this switch, a relay in the gimbal control was energised and locked. When this occurred, power was removed from the roll repeater motor and the roll repeater was then capable of providing a reference point for the roll gimbal. A good example of the time when this facility may be required is reported below.

On 18 November 1960, a thick blanket of autumn evening fog covered the Lincolnshire countryside. The ORB for 106 Squadron at Bardney reported that a phase two limited dry countdown on Pad 19 was successful, but that there was no LRT capture due to the visibility being only 20 yards. An issue with the long-range theodolite in particular was that of visibility. The distance between the LRT and the missile was considerable, 425 feet (129.5 metres), the intervening atmosphere needing to be clear enough for the LRT to see the prism in the guidance system.

The fog did not necessarily have to be naturally formed. In addition to poor visibility caused by meteorological phenomena, fog could also be caused by the activity surrounding the missile itself. When fuelled, the LOX would boil off and vent from the right-hand side of the missile near to the top of the LOX tank. If the air mass surrounding the area was moist, mixing with the vented LOX would cause excess water vapour to condense out into visible water droplets, hence, Thor could produce its own localised fog at the pad.

The issues surrounding poor visibility and LRT capture were not limited to Thor. Concerns in this area prompted the US Army Missile Command at the Redstone Arsenal in Alabama, via the Department of the Navy, to contract with the Visibility Laboratory at the University of California for the conduct of a study into the problems associated with the optical alignment of missiles in restricted visibility conditions, such as those caused by fog. Some work had already been carried out on methods of dispersing or simply penetrating natural fogs and fog condensates resulting from the pre-launch fuelling of a missile with LOX. These methods were reviewed and experiments conducted using polarisation techniques for the suppression of unwanted back-scattered light in one existing optical alignment theodolite system—that in use for Thor's sister, Jupiter. Some alternative methods to optical alignment were also suggested, such as microwave interferometry, and although this was thought to be a possibly viable alternative, work proceeded on the solution to the optical problem.

Short-range theodolites were not an issue as, due to the much shorter distances involved, solutions were available—such as surrounding the optical path with a tube that could then be purged free of any fog by the injection of a 'dry' atmosphere (for example, nitrogen) at low velocity to minimise turbulence.

The reason that fog affected the theodolites was that it constitutes a transmission medium that has prominent light-scattering properties. The scattering process reduced the signal to noise ratio of the error signals and significantly reduced theodolite performance.

The conclusion of the study was that no statistically significant improvement of the theodolite system in foggy conditions was achieved.

Despite extensive searches on both sides of the Atlantic, the author has been unable to access imagery of the actual Thor system LRT, the requests for information triggering, from certain quarters, some very interesting reactions.

Guidance Countdown

The guidance countdown is reproduced below. It should be noted that, although the loops (circuits) for a certain piece of the equipment may be closed during a particular alignment step, the equipment itself may not necessarily commence its function until a subsequent align step is entered. Diagrams of the alignment set components, along with a brief description of their function, follow the guidance countdown notes.

General

The guidance system countdown can operate in either 'normal' or 'manual' modes. In either mode, it has the following sequence: off, standby, power on, align step one, align step two, align step three, and complete. There is also provision for guidance stop.

Off

There is distribution of 28V DC main power. As an indication of this distribution, the GSE 28V DC lamp provided on the accelerometer control would be illuminated.

Standby

Ground support equipment (GSE) 115V single-phase 60-Hz AC and inertial guidance equipment (IGE) 115V three-phase 400-Hz AC power distribution loops would be closed, making that power available to its associated equipment. The GSE 115V 60-Hz lamp will be illuminated on the accelerometer control and the illumination of lamps provided on the indicator control voltage readout, RD 184 recorder plotter and the MX 2370 counter indicate that this loop is closed and power is being fed. The IGE 115V three-phase 400-Hz power will cause the IGE 'A' and 'C' lamps to be illuminated on the accelerometer control indicating that this loop is also complete.

Power On

In this mode, the following alignment set loops are closed. Inertial guidance equipment 28V DC power distribution: relays operate within the airborne guidance set, routing power to the elements of the guidance set which receive power during this phase. GSE 115V 400-Hz three-power distribution loop: GSE A, B, and C lamps will illuminate on the accelerometer control. GSE 270V DC power distribution loop: an illuminated GSE B+ lamp on the accelerometer control will signal that this power distribution loop is complete. Voltage and signal monitoring loops: these loops monitor the distribution of voltage and signals within the alignment set components and also the airborne guidance set. The voltages and signals so monitored are 115V 60-Hz single-phase main power, 115V 400-Hz three-phase main power, 28V DC main power, 270V DC output of the PP-1917 power supply, 270V DC output from the guidance set, 28V DC input to the guidance set, 115V 400-Hz three-phase output of PU-411 motor generator, and 35V 400-Hz single-phase precision power output of the PP-1811 power supply in the airborne guidance set, yaw steering signals and pitch steering signals, also from the airborne guidance set. Gyro heater power monitoring loops: the gyro heater power monitoring loops monitor the distribution of the 115V 400-Hz three-phase power supply for the stabilisation and accelerometer gyros in the airborne guidance set. Distribution of this power is indicated by the cyclic illumination of lamps on the theodolite amplifier. Gimbal angle repeater loops: these loops indicate the alignment of the inertial platform. The loops receive the output signals from the roll, yaw, and pitch gimbal transmitter synchros in the airborne guidance set. The signals are routed through mixer amplifiers and position repeater amplifiers to the gimbal position indicator drive motors. The motors drive control transformer rotors to drive the gimbal position indicators. Stabilisation gyro output meter loops: the stabilisation gyro output meter loops indicate the outputs of the stabilisation gyro signal microsyns. The outputs of the X, Y, and Z stabilisation gyros are routed through the null meter amplifier to the stab gyro output meters. Stabilisation torque amplifier loops: these loops maintain the alignment of the stabilised platform by using the outputs of the stabilisation gyros and the earth rate and gyro unbalance correction signals. In the erection integrator, the signals control a motor, which positions the wiper arm of a potentiometer to produce an output that cancels the effect of the earth's rotation and gyro unbalance on the loops.

Align Step One

In the align step one mode, the following loops are closed. Azimuth mirror drive loops: the azimuth mirror drive loops align the movable mirror located in the platform group of the guidance set. Alignment null meter loops: these loops indicate elevation and the horizontal and azimuth alignment of the stabilised platform. The pitch axis null, roll axis null, and yaw axis null meters provided on the gimbal control indicate the output of the vertical sensing element. With the HOR attitude switch is pressed, the pitch axis null and roll axis null meters register the outputs of the VSE, and the yaw axis null meter registers the output of the short-range theodolite. When the VERT attitude switch is pressed, loops are closed that direct the VSE outputs to the pitch axis null meter and the yaw axis null meters, while the roll axis null meter registers the output of the long-range theodolite. Gimbal alignment loops: The gimbal alignment loops are provided for driving the roll, yaw, and pitch gimbals to achieve alignment of the stabilised platform. Signals from the transmitter synchros on the roll, yaw, and pitch gimbals are routed to control transformers on the gimbal position indicators and are then fed into mixer amplifiers. Any misalignment of the stabilised platform would result in the generation of error signals, which would cause the gimbals to be driven in the required direction to achieve alignment.

Align Step Two

In align step two, the following alignment set loops are closed. Gimbal angle position tachometer return loops: these loops filter and amplify the outputs of the tachometers that are geared to the motors which drive the gimbals of the stabilised platform. Vertical sensing element alignment loops: the VSE alignment loops maintain alignment of the stabilised platform in the pitch and roll axes by means of the outputs from the vertical sensing element. With the HOR attitude switch operated, the output of the VSE is routed to the pitch and roll loops. In the pitch loop, the VSE output passes through a null signal amplifier to the pitch axis null meter and then on to a mixer amplifier. In the roll loop, the VSE output passes through a null signal amplifier to the roll axis null meter and on to a mixer amplifier. When the VERT switch is operated, the VSE outputs are routed to the pitch and yaw loops. The pitch loop remains the same for both the horizontal and the vertical attitudes of the missile. In the yaw loop, the output of the VSE is sent via a null signal amplifier to the yaw axis null meter and then on to the mixer amplifier. Gyro accelerometer repeater loops: the gyro accelerometer repeater loops indicate the rate of rotation of the accelerometer gyros. The signal indicating the rate of rotation of the gyros is applied to a control transformer in the gyro accelerometer repeater in the accelerometer control. Any errors in the speed of rotation of the accelerometer gyros will cause an error signal that is amplified in the accelerometer repeater amplifier and routed to the gyro accelerometer repeater drive motor. This motor is also geared to the control transformer, so that when the repeater motor reaches a speed proportional to the rotation of the accelerometer gyro, the error signal is nulled. Accelerometer gyro response test loops: the accelerometer gyro response test loops check the operation of the accelerometer gyro nulling loops. Accelerometer gyro null adjustment loops: these loops supply the accelerometer gyro nulling loops with voltages that cancel the effects of gravity. The voltages are produced by the accelerometer gyro null adjustment potentiometers. The supplied signals are monitored on the accelerometer loop null meter on the accelerometer control panel. Electro-theodolite channel loops: these loops distribute SRT power to AC lamps (6.3V), pre-amplifier AC (270V), pre-amplifier AC filament power (6.3V), glow tube DC (270V), the output of the modulator section to the SRT, and, finally, any azimuth deviation signals to the theodolite amplifier. The theodolite channel output can be observed on the roll axis null meter if the missile is vertical or on the yaw axis null meter should the missile be in the horizontal attitude. Velocity calibrator loops: the velocity calibrator loops permit the guidance control to set the airborne guidance set Vg potentiometer shafts. When the guidance control X channel, Y channel, and Z channel counter transmitter synchros are set, error signals are produced by the receiver synchros for the corresponding channels in the airborne guidance set. These error signals are utilised to drive the Vg potentiometers. The engine cut-off signals that result from this illuminate the lamps (computer near zero; computer on zero) at the guidance control. Vg clutch control loops: the Vg clutch control loops permit the guidance control to energise or de-energise the Vg potentiometer loops. The guidance control is provided with a switch marked computer adjust and lock for each computer channel. If the switches are set to lock, the clutches in the airborne guidance set are energised. The counters in the guidance control X, Y, and Z channels can be operated. Launch control yaw slewing group: the launch control yaw slewing group checks the operation of the loops, which permit the guidance control to drive and monitor the yaw gimbal in the airborne guidance set. The guidance control is provided with yaw gimbal slew switches. Signals from the slew switches in the guidance control are routed to the gimbal control. The output from the gimbal control transformer is then routed through a position repeater amplifier to a motor, which then drives the yaw angle indicator and transmitter synchro. The transmitter synchro in the yaw angle indicator in the gimbal control is connected to synchros in both the airborne guidance set and the guidance control. As a result of the transmitter synchro in the gimbal control being moved, an error signal is produced in the other synchros. In respect of the guidance control, the error signal produced is utilised to drive the yaw gimbal angle indicator. Once the yaw gimbal has been driven to a position that causes a null of the synchro error signals, the guidance control yaw gimbal angle indicator and the gimbal control yaw angle indicator will indicate the gimbal angle.

Align Step Three

During this step, the following alignment set component loops are closed: stabilisation gyro response test; align step three mode alignment null meter; auxiliary azimuth erection integrator repeater; auxiliary stabilisation torque amplifier; velocity zero direction meter; and velocity calibrator loops. Stabilisation gyro response test loops: the stabilisation gyro response test loops are used to check the correct operation of the stabilisation gyro nulling loops. Align step three mode alignment null meter loops: these loops indicate the elevation and the horizontal and azimuth alignment of the stabilised platform. The loops operate in the same manner as the alignment null meter loops, which are closed in the align step one mode. These checks are repeated only to ensure that the loops continue to work properly in the align step three mode. Auxiliary azimuth erection integrator repeater loops: these loops resolve the auxiliary azimuth alignment control signals. Auxiliary azimuth stabilisation torque amplifier loops: these loops maintain the alignment of the stabilised platform during auxiliary azimuth conditions. It is the output of the VSE that maintains alignment in this mode. When the VERT switch is pressed, the VSE output is routed through two loops. In the first, the signal is processed through a resolver drive amplifier and sent to the resolver synchro in the pitch angle indicator. The resolver synchro output is routed to the Y stabilisation torque amplifier and to the Y erection integrator amplifier and on to the motor which drives the wiper arm of the Y erection integrator potentiometer. The motor positions the wiper arm so that a voltage is produced which cancels the effect of the earth's rotation and any gyro unbalance. In the second loop, the signal is applied to the Z stabilisation torque amplifier, the Z erection integrator amplifier and the motor that drives the wiper arm of the Z erection integrator potentiometer. The wiper arm is positioned such that a voltage is produced that cancels the effect of the earth's rotation and any gyro unbalance. When the HOR switch is pressed, the signal routing is essentially the same as that described for the vertical case, the only difference being that the signals are routed through loops to the X and Z stabilisation torque amplifiers. Direction to zero meter loops: the direction to zero meter loops indicate the direction in which the Vg potentiometers must be driven in order to reach zero settings. The Vg potentiometer output signals can be monitored on the direction to zero meter on the velocity control. Velocity calibrator loops: the velocity calibrator loops position the Vg potentiometer shafts in the guidance set. The signals which position the Vg potentiometer shafts are produced by transmitter synchros geared to the three velocity calibrators in the velocity control.

Complete Mode

In this mode, the following loops are closed: complete mode stabilisation torque amplifier; airframe azimuth reference; and emergency stop loops. Complete mode stabilisation torque amplifier loops: the complete mode stabilisation torque amplifier loops supply the stabilised platform alignment loops with a constant voltage that cancels the effect of the earth's rotation and also the effects of any gyro unbalance. During the align step three mode, the wiper arms of the erection integrator potentiometers were driven by motors to a position where this voltage was produced and now the wiper arms remain in this position as the input supply to the motors is removed. Airframe azimuth reference loop: this loop, as its name implies, references the roll gimbal to the missile airframe. The loop is activated by pressing the 'airframe az. ref.' switch. The integral lamp will light to indicate that the loop is active. Upon pressing this switch, a relay in the gimbal control is energised and locked. When this occurs, power is removed from the roll repeater motor and the roll repeater is then capable of providing a reference point for the roll gimbal. Guidance stop loops: the guidance stop loops will return the guidance alignment set to the standby normal mode. The loops are closed by pressing the guidance stop switch (alignment control or guidance control). A guidance stop lamp will illuminate to indicate operation of the switch. The reset switch will permit the alignment set to be operated after the guidance stop switch has been pressed. Pressing the reset switch will extinguish the guidance stop lamp and illuminate the standby lamp. Automatic guidance stop: the automatic guidance stop loops protect the stabilised platform gimbals from damage. Should the system detect a gimbal tumbling condition, sensed from the increased magnitude of a tachometer output signal, a series of relay operations take place which will interrupt the power supply to the power distribution relays and the system is reversed to a guidance stop condition. Timed sequence circuit: the timed sequence circuit will automatically advance the guidance system through the alignment modes from power on to the align step two mode. The system is operated by pressing the timed countdown switch (switch and lamp on alignment control, toggle switch on guidance control) when the system is in standby mode. When operating, the timed sequence circuit will supply power to an electronic timer, which in turn controls the supply to a ledex stepping switch. The system will operate so that the guidance countdown progresses to align step two mode. Approximately fifty seconds after the system has advanced to the align step two mode, the advance lamp will illuminate to indicate that the system can be advanced to the align step three mode. Approximately 145 seconds after the system has been advanced to the align step three mode, the advance lamp will once again illuminate to indicate that the system may be advanced to the complete mode.

Electronic Timing Circuit

Timing interval one (fifteen seconds): this interval is the period of progression from the power on mode to the align step one mode. Timing interval two (fifteen seconds): this interval is the period of progression from the align step one mode to the align step two mode. Timing interval three (fifty seconds): this interval begins when the guidance system has reached align step two. When this interval times out, the advance lamp will illuminate, indicating that the system can be advanced to the align step three mode. Timing interval four (145 Seconds): this interval begins when the guidance system has been advanced to the align step three. When this interval times out, the advance lamp will illuminate, indicating that the system can be advanced to the complete mode.

Vertical Hold Loop

The vertical hold loop maintains the system in the vertical attitude from the align step one mode through to the complete mode. The loop is operated by pressing the VERT switch (alignment control and guidance control). When the switch is pressed, the integral lamp signalling the operation of the loop will illuminate. The switch, when pressed, routes 28V DC power to relays in the gimbal control to maintain the system in vertical condition.

Guidance Control

The guidance control consisted of two circuits, the velocity calibrator circuit and the Vg potentiometer circuit. It also performed the following major functions: drive and monitor the yaw gimbal in the guidance set, monitor stabilised platform alignment, indicate the progression through the guidance countdown modes, and provide for guidance stop.

Function of Controls and Indicators
Direction to Zero Meter and Channel Switch
This instrument registered in the opposite direction to the negative or positive outputs of the Vgx, Vgy, or Vgz potentiometer as selected on the channel selector switch. It thus supplied 'command' information, indicating the adjustment required to bring the selected channel to zero.

Computer Near Zero (X channel)
The computer near zero lamp signalled the approximate zero position of the Vgx potentiometer shaft and the operation of the main engine cut-off switch.

Computer on Zero (X Channel)
The computer on zero on lamp signalled the zero position of the Vgx potentiometer and the operation of the vernier engine cut-off switch.

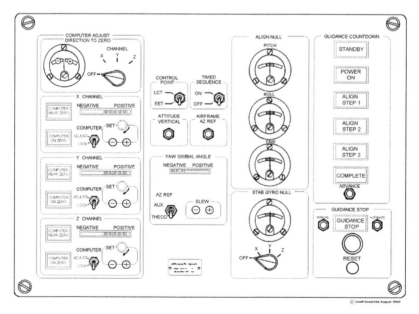

GUIDANCE CONTROL

Counter (X Channel)
The counter showed the setting of the Vgx potentiometer transmitter synchro.

Computer Switch (X Channel)
This switch energised or de-energised the electromagnetic clutch on the Vgx potentiometer shaft. When set to adjust, the clutch was de-energised. When set to lock, the clutch was energised.

Set Control (X Channel)
This rotary control set the rotor of the Vgx potentiometer transmitter synchro to exact alignment.

Slew Switches (X Channel)
These switches set the rotor of the Vgx potentiometer to coarse alignment.

Computer Near Zero (Y Channel)
The computer near zero lamp signalled the approximate zero position of the Vgy potentiometer shaft.

Computer on Zero (Y Channel)
The computer on zero on lamp signalled the zero position of the Vgy potentiometer shaft.

Counter (Y Channel)
The counter showed the setting of the Vgy potentiometer transmitter synchro.

Computer Switch (Y Channel)
This switch energised or de-energised the electromagnetic clutch on the Vgy potentiometer shaft. When set to adjust, the clutch was de-energised. When set to lock, the clutch was energised.

Set Control (Y Channel)
This rotary control set the rotor of the Vgy potentiometer transmitter synchro to exact alignment.

Slew Switches (Y Channel)
These switches set the rotor of the Vgy potentiometer to coarse alignment.

Computer Near Zero (Z channel)
The computer near zero lamp signalled the approximate zero position of the Vgz potentiometer shaft.

Computer on Zero (Z Channel)

The computer on zero on lamp signalled the zero position of the Vgz potentiometer shaft.

Counter (Z Channel)

The counter showed the setting of the Vgz potentiometer transmitter synchro.

Computer Switch (Z Channel)

This switch energised or de-energised the electromagnetic clutch on the Vgz potentiometer shaft. When set to adjust, the clutch was de-energised. When set to lock, the clutch was energised.

Set Control (Z Channel)

This rotary control set the rotor of the Vgz potentiometer transmitter synchro to exact alignment.

Slew Switches (Z Channel)

These switches set the rotor of the Vgz potentiometer to coarse alignment.

Control Point

This switch sets the guidance set control point to either the launching control group (LCT) or the launching countdown group (EET).

Timed Sequence

This switch controlled the timed sequence circuit. The circuit automatically advanced the system from the power on mode to the align step two mode. After selection, the power on lamps would illuminate, and after fifteen seconds, the align step one lamp would light. After a further fifteen-second interval, the align step two lamp illuminated.

Attitude Vertical Switch

This combined switch and lamp indicated the selection of the vertical missile attitude

Airframe Azimuth Reference

The airframe azimuth switch and lamp selected and indicated that the roll gimbal was referenced to the missile airframe.

Yaw Gimbal Angle

This small panel permitted the guidance control to drive and monitor the yaw gimbal in the airborne guidance set. The yaw gimbal slew was produced by operating the slew switches on this panel. The position of the yaw gimbal could be read on the yaw gimbal angle indicator. The switch marked 'az. ref.' determined the azimuth reference to long-range theodolite, short-range theodolite, or auxiliary reference, which is the output from the VSE.

Align Null Meters
These meters indicated the elevation, horizontal, and azimuth alignment of the stabilised platform.

Stab Gyro Null Meter and Channel Selector Switch
This meter indicated the output of the stabilisation gyros as selected by the channel selector switch.

Guidance Countdown Lamps
The illumination of these lamps indicated the progression of the alignment set through the guidance countdown modes.

Advance Switch
This switch and lamp combination advanced the alignment set to the next mode. It is also indicated that the alignment set could be advanced to align step three and complete modes during the timed sequence countdown operation.

Guidance Stop Lamp
This lamp indicated that the alignment set had been returned to the standby mode.

Guidance Stop Switch
This switch returned the alignment set to the standby mode.

Reset Switch
The use of this switch permitted the alignment set to be operated after the guidance stop switch has been pressed.

Automatic Guidance Stop Switch and Lamp
This combined lamp and switch selected and indicated the automatic guidance stop mode. The circuit received tachometer outputs from the stabilised platform. When this output was of a magnitude large enough to indicate a 'gimbal tumble' condition, the gimbal tumbling sensing circuit in the theodolite amplifier activated the guidance stop circuit.

Manual Guidance Stop switch and Lamp
This combined lamp and switch selected and indicated that the guidance stop circuit was in the manual mode.

Guidance Alignment Set Components

RD 184 Recorder

The RD 184 recorder consisted of three sub-assemblies: a switch to select the circuit to be monitored; the circuitry to inject a test signal into the circuit being monitored; and a recording device used to monitor the response of the circuit or unit under test. The response was recorded on a moving paper chart. The RD 184 recorder was used to time the response of the X, Y, and Z accelerometer gyro loops and the X, Y, and Z stabilisation gyro loops.

Function of Controls and Indicators

Power On Switch

The main power switch for this unit caused each stylus to be heated in order to prevent the stylus sticking to the paper when the unit record switch was set to on.

Pulse Check Switch

This switch applied a gyro test signal to the MX2370 counter for a pulse width check.

Marker Interval Switch

The marker stylus remained at the upper edge of the recording graph paper at all times. When this switch was set to continuous, the stylus produced a 60-Hz trace at the top of the recording paper. On the 'one/sec' position, the stylus was energised at one-second intervals. This function was used for measuring paper speed.

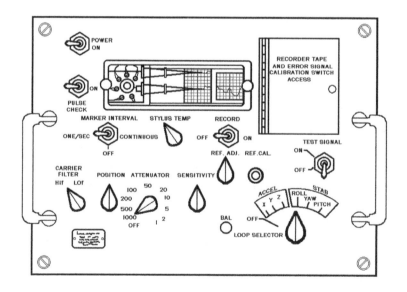

RD - 184 Recorder

Stylus Temp Switch
This switch controlled the temperature of the stylus.

Plotter
This device consisted of graph paper moving at 1 inch per second and over which the stylus recorded.

Record Switch
With the record switch at 'on', the paper drive and paper take-up motors were energised, causing the graph paper to move across the writing surface.

Carrier Filter Switch
This switch controlled the frequency response of the filter, which filtered the monitored signal.

Position Control
This control positioned the stylus on the graph paper.

Attenuator
This controlled the height of the graph trace by attenuating the monitored signal.

Sensitivity Control
Controlled the sensitivity of the RD 184 recorder unit.

Reference Adjustment Control
This adjusted the amount of stylus deflection for calibration purposes.

Reference Calibration Switch
This applied a deflection voltage to the stylus during calibration.

Test Signal Switch
This applied a test signal to the gyro loop selected for monitoring.

Loop Selector
This selected the output of the gyro to be monitored on the plotter.

Bal
This was a plate allowing access to the potentiometer adjustment shaft for balancing purposes.

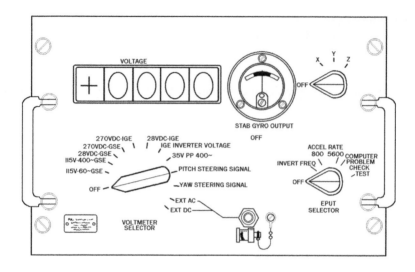

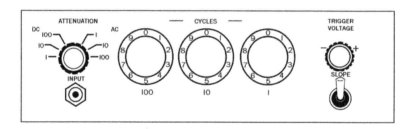

Indicator Control

The indicator control monitored voltages and indicated the stabilisation gyro outputs. It also selected the inputs to the MX-2370 counter. The pre-determined counter started and stopped the MX-2370 counter during inverter frequency and accelerometer rate checks.

Function of Controls and Indicators

Voltage Readout
This indicated the voltage that had been selected for monitoring by the voltmeter selector.

Stab Gyro Output Meter
This meter indicated the output of the X, Y, or Z stabilisation gyro as selected.

Stab Gyro Output Selector
This switch selected the X, Y, or Z stabilisation gyro output for monitoring on the stab gyro output meter.

Voltmeter Selector
This rotary switch selected the source of the voltage for monitoring on the voltage readout.

EPUT (Events Per Unit Time) Meter
This switch selected the inputs to the predetermined counter and provided external control of the MX-2370 counter relays.

Pre-determined Counter

Attenuation Selector
Controlled the attenuation of the signal being applied to the predetermined counter.

Input Jack
This jack was used for connecting a signal to the predetermined counter.

Readout
This provided a visual indication of the operation of the predetermined counter.

Trigger Voltage Control
This controlled the voltage at which attenuated signals triggered the pre-determined counter input trigger channel.

Slope Switch
This switch selected one of two outputs from the pre-determined counter input trigger channel.

Theodolite Amplifier

The theodolite amplifier performed the following functions: controlled the short-range theodolite azimuth alignment loop, controlled the 115V 400-Hz three-phase power and the 28V DC power circuits, monitored the gyro heater power, provided fuse protection for system power, and provided an automatic guidance stop signal when gimbal tumbling occurred.

Function of Controls and Indicators
Accelerometer Lamps
The accelerometer lamps signalled the operation of the X, Y, and Z accelerometer gyro heaters as appropriate.

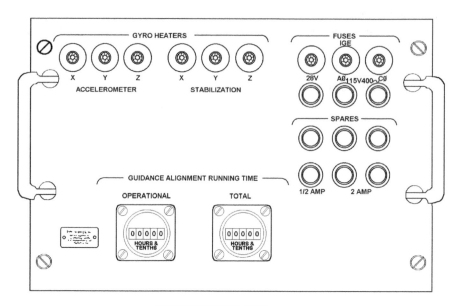

THEODOLITE AMPLIFIER

Stabilisation Lamps
These lamps signalled the operation of the X, Y, and Z stabilisation gyro heaters as appropriate.

28V, A Phase and C Phase Lamps
These lamps illuminated to signal that the associated fuse had blown.

Spares
Spare ½ amp (2) and two amp fuses (4).

Elapsed Time Indicators
Total
This elapsed time indicator recorded, in hours and tenths of an hour, the time that 115V 60-Hz GSE (ground support equipment) power had been applied to the alignment set.

Operational
This indicator recorded, in hours and tenths of an hour, the time that 115V 400-Hz three-phase GSE power had been applied to the alignment set.

Alignment Control

The alignment control consisted of switching circuits and indication lamp circuits, which controlled and indicated alignment set mode operation.

Function of Controls and Indicators

Target Lamps
Indicated target one or target two as selected by the target switch.

Target Switch
This switch operated a target select relay to route Vg potentiometer outputs across the target one or target two 'Q' potentiometers.

Control Point Lamps
The illumination of these lamps indicated that the guidance set control point was in either the launching control group (LCT) or the launching countdown group (EET) trailers.

Countdown Sequence
These combined switch and lamp units selected and indicated, as appropriate, the manual or timed progression through the modes.

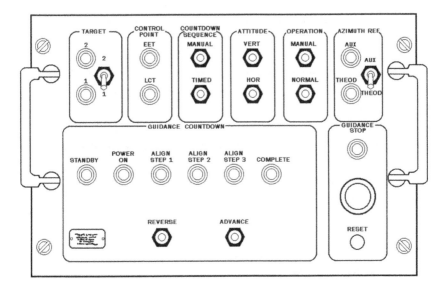

ALIGNMENT CONTROL

Attitude Switches and Lamps
These switches and lamps indicated the selection of the horizontal missile attitude loop operation or the vertical missile attitude loop operation.

Operation
These combined switches and lamps were utilised to select and signal normal or manual loop operation as appropriate.

Azimuth Reference
The lamps signalled the selection of the associated switch. In the theodolite position of the switch, operation of the short-range theodolite or long-range theodolite loops is indicated. In the auxiliary position, auxiliary azimuth is selected. In this condition, the stabilised platform alignment was maintained by the VSE.

Guidance Countdown Lamps
The illumination of these lamps indicated the progression of the alignment set through the guidance countdown modes.

Advance Switch
The guidance countdown circuit controlled the operation of a Ledex stepping switch. The circuit consisted of switches and relays which applied or removed control signals from the Ledex switch. The 'ADVANCE' switch energised a relay that, in turn, routed 28V DC power to the motor, which advanced the Ledex switch. This switch and lamp combination advanced the alignment set to the next mode and indicated that alignment set could be advanced to align step three and complete modes during the timed sequence countdown operation.

Reverse Switch
This switch was used to return the alignment set to the preceding mode.
The 'REVERSE' switch applied 28V DC to a motor, which reversed the Ledex switch.

Guidance Stop Lamp
This lamp indicated that the alignment set had been returned to the standby mode.

Guidance Stop Switch
This switch returns the alignment set to the standby mode.

Reset Switch
The use of this switch permitted the alignment set to be operated after the guidance stop switch had been pressed.

Gimbal Control

The gimbal control performed the following functions: airframe azimuth reference, monitored the stabilised platform alignment, controlled the stabilised platform alignment, controlled the gimbal position indicator slewing voltage, and relayed signals.

Function of Controls and Indicators
Pitch, Yaw, and Roll Axis Meters
These meters measured the outputs of the associated loops and showed the pitch, roll, and azimuth alignment of the stabilised platform.

Pitch Axis Null Meter
This meter indicated the output of the VSE.

Yaw Axis Null Meter
With the HOR attitude switch (alignment control) pressed, this meter indicated the output of the short-range theodolite; with the VERT attitude switch pressed, the meter indicated the output of the VSE.

Roll Axis Null Meter
With the HOR attitude switch pressed, this meter indicated the output of the VSE; with the VERT attitude switch pressed, the meter indicated the output of the long-range theodolite.

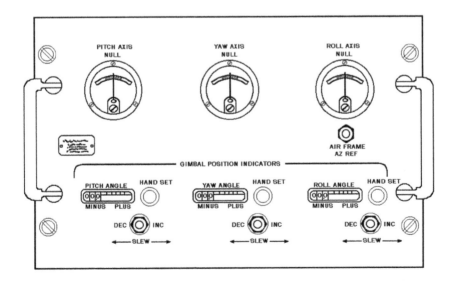

GIMBAL CONTROL

Airframe Azimuth Reference Switch and Lamp
The switch selected and the lamp signalled that the missile airframe was being used for roll gimbal reference.

Gimbal Position Indicator Circuits
The gimbal position indicator circuits showed the stabilised platform alignment by registering the outputs of the transmitter synchros. The transmitter synchro outputs, when applied to the receiver synchros in the gimbal control, produced error signals that were sent through amplifiers and position repeater amplifiers to the motors, which would drive the receiver synchros and the gimbal position indicators.

Pitch, Yaw, and Roll Angle Indicator
These indicated the setting of the appropriate gimbal angle repeater synchro.

Pitch, Yaw, and Roll Angle Slew Switch
These switches were used to drive the appropriate angle indicator to their coarse settings.

Pitch, Yaw, and Roll Hand Set Control
These switches provided manual adjustment for refining the appropriate gimbal angle indicator setting.

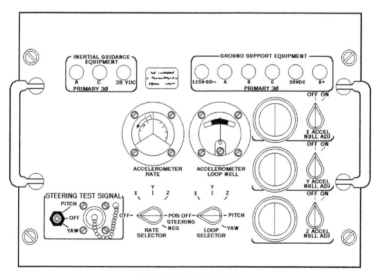

ACCELEROMETER CONTROL

Accelerometer Control

The accelerometer control circuits performed the following functions: null the accelerometer gyros, monitored the accelerometer gyro signal microsyn outputs, monitored the distribution of system power, monitored the accelerometer gyro rate of rotation, provided a voltage for the high-g nulling test, and routed signals within the accelerometer control and alignment set.

Function of Controls and Indicators

Inertial Guidance Equipment Power Lamps
These lamps indicated that A phase, C phase (primary three-phase) and 28V DC power was being supplied to the airborne guidance set.

Ground Support Equipment Power Lamps
These lamps indicated that 115V 60 Hz, A phase, B phase, C phase (primary three-phase), 28V DC, and B+ power was being applied to the ground-support equipment.

Accelerometer Rate Indicator
This meter indicated whether the accelerometer gyro (as selected) was rotating, and if so, at what rate of rotation.

Rate Selector Switch
This rotary switch selected the output of the X, Y, or Z accelerometer gyro for monitoring on the accelerometer rate indicator.

Accelerometer Loop Null Meter
This meter indicated the output of the X, Y, or Z accelerometer gyro, as selected. If the gyro was rotating at the correct rate, the meter would be showing a null output from the accelerometer gyro microsyns.

Loop Selector Switch
This rotary switch selected the output of the X, Y, or Z accelerometer gyro for monitoring on the accelerometer loop null meter.

X, Y, and Z Accelerometer Null Adjustment Control
These rotary controls set the X, Y, and Z accelerometer gyro null adjustment potentiometers. The control routed signals to the guidance set which, rotated the appropriate accelerometer gyro at the proper rate to null the output of the signal microsyns.

X, Y, and Z Null Adjustment Switch
These switches opened or closed the circuits carrying the X, Y, or Z null adjustment potentiometer output.

Steering Test Signal Jack
The jack provided an outlet for monitoring the steering test signals as selected by
the steering test signals switch.

Steering Test Signal Switch
This switch selected the steering test signal to be applied to the steering test signal
jack. This was used to test the high-g nulling capabilities of the accelerometer
gyros.

Azimuth Control

The azimuth control circuits aligned the movable mirror in the platform group of
the guidance set and amplified signals, which aligned the stabilised platform.

Function of Controls and Indicators
Mirror Angle Setting Indicator
This indicated the setting of the mirror angle synchro.

Hand Set Control
This rotary control provided manual adjustment for refining the setting of the
mirror angle setting indicator.

Slew Switch
The slew switch was used to drive the mirror angle setting indicator to coarse
setting.

Velocity Control

The velocity control consists of the velocity calibrator circuit, Vg potentiometer
circuit, power control circuit, and the computer problem check circuit.

Function of Controls and Indicators
Accelerator Torque Signal Switch
This applied 'Q' Vg signals to the accelerometer gyro microsyns.

Direction to Zero Meter and Channel Switch
This instrument registered in the opposite direction to the negative or positive
outputs of the Vgx, Vgy, or Vgz potentiometer as selected on the channel selector
switch. It thus supplied command information, indicating the adjustment required
to bring the selected channel to zero.

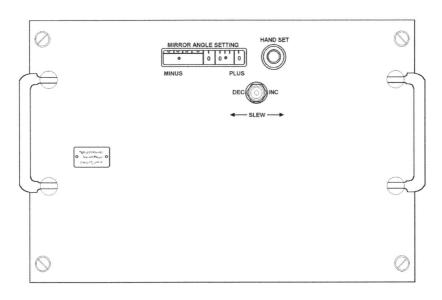

AZIMUTH CONTROL

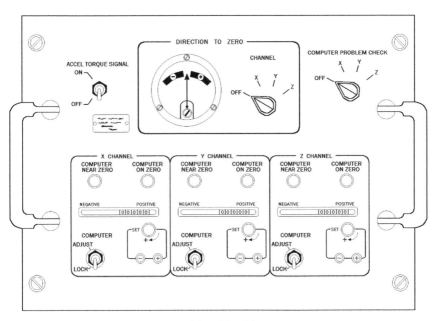

VELOCITY CONTROL

Computer Problem Check
This switch selected the output of the Vgx, Vgy, or Vgz potentiometer for monitoring.

Computer Near Zero (X channel)
The computer near zero lamp signalled the approximate zero position of the Vgx potentiometer shaft and the operation of the main engine cut-off switch.

Computer on Zero (X Channel)
The computer on zero on lamp signalled the zero position of the Vgx potentiometer and the operation of the vernier engine cut-off switch.

Counter (X Channel)
The counter showed the setting of the Vgx potentiometer transmitter synchro.

Computer Switch (X Channel)
This switch energised or de-energised the electromagnetic clutch on the Vgx potentiometer shaft. When set to adjust, the clutch was de-energised. When set to lock, the clutch was energised.

Set Control (X Channel)
This rotary control set the rotor of the Vgx potentiometer transmitter synchro to exact alignment.

Slew Switches (X Channel)
These switches set the rotor of the Vgx potentiometer to coarse alignment.

Computer Near Zero (Y Channel)
The computer near zero lamp signalled the approximate zero position of the Vgy potentiometer shaft.

Computer on Zero (Y Channel)
The computer on zero on lamp signalled the zero position of the Vgy potentiometer shaft.

Counter (Y Channel)
The counter showed the setting of the Vgy potentiometer transmitter synchro.

Computer Switch (Y Channel)
This switch energised or de-energised the electromagnetic clutch on the Vgy potentiometer shaft. When set to adjust, the clutch was de-energised. When set to lock, the clutch was energised.

Set Control (Y Channel)
This rotary control set the rotor of the Vgy potentiometer transmitter synchro to exact alignment.

Slew Switches (Y Channel)
These switches set the rotor of the Vgy potentiometer to coarse alignment.

Computer Near Zero (Z channel)
The computer near zero lamp signalled the approximate zero position of the Vgz potentiometer shaft.

Computer on Zero (Z Channel)
The computer on zero on lamp signalled the zero position of the Vgz potentiometer shaft.

Counter (Z Channel)
The counter showed the setting of the Vgz potentiometer transmitter synchro.

Computer Switch (Z Channel)
This switch energised or de-energised the electromagnetic clutch on the Vgz potentiometer shaft. When set to adjust, the clutch was de-energised. When set to lock, the clutch was energised.

Set Control (Z Channel)
This rotary control set the rotor of the Vgz potentiometer transmitter synchro to exact alignment.

Slew Switches (Z Channel)
These switches set the rotor of the Vgz potentiometer to coarse alignment.

Erection Control

Erection integrator repeaters in the erection control provided voltages, which cancelled the effects of the earth's rotation and gyro unbalance in the stabilisation loops.

Function of Controls and Indicators
X Axis Indicator
This instrument indicated the torque applied to the X stabilisation float to cancel the effect of the earth's rotation.

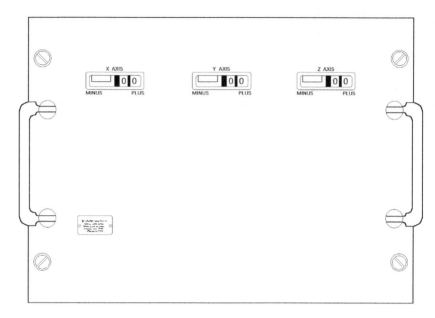

ERECTION CONTROL

Y Axis Indicator
This instrument indicated the torque applied to the Y stabilisation float to cancel the effect of the earth's rotation.

Z Axis Indicator
This instrument indicated the torque applied to the Z stabilisation float to cancel the effect of the earth's rotation.
    The following panels had blank front faces and are therefore not illustrated.

Digital Voltmeter
The digital voltmeter was an electronic voltmeter that displayed the value of an input voltage in digital form. It was capable of measuring either DC or AC voltages accurately to four significant figures. Accuracy was plus-one digit for DC voltages and plus-two digits for AC voltages.

PP-1917 Power Supply
The PP-1917 power supply converted a 115V 400-Hz three-phase input into 270V DC and 150V DC outputs.

Theodolite Panel
The theodolite panel circuits provided filament power for the short-range theodolite and routed power and signals. The input was 115V 60-Hz AC and this

was converted to the 6.3V filament power. There were two 6.3V outputs, one output to the lamps on the back of the short-range theodolite and the other for filament power to the SRT pre-amplifiers.

The power and signal routing circuits routed power and signals to the alignment set components. The 'TARGET' switch on the alignment control controlled a relay that routed power to the target one and target two lamps.

Voltage Regulator

The voltage regulator provided a regulated 115V 60-HZ single-phase output, which was used for filament power, operating voltage, and reference voltage for the alignment set components. The output of the regulator maintained the voltage to 115V plus 4 per cent.

All panel drawings are by the author.

4

The Launch Control Area

The Launch Control Area

The position of the launch control area (LCA) in relation to the emplacements varied from site to site, but it was generally situated a distance in the region of 700 feet (213 metres) from the nearest missile. Essentially, the LCA was a right-angled triangle with the acute angles removed, the resulting irregular pentagon giving the area its distinctive form, still visible at many sites today and covering an area of approximately 1,142 square yards (955 square metres).

The LCA was the location of the LCT, the PDT, and the three trailer-mounted diesel engine generator sets. The only permanent structure on the LCA was a fuel oil catch pit and supports for the 5,000-gallon (22,700-litre) capacity diesel tank supplying the generators. The trailers were connected via cabling trenches, having concrete covers flush with the surface. The RAF added a local modification to the original LCA equipment in the form of an annex to the LCT. A terrapin building, measuring 22 feet × 18 feet (6.7 × 5.5 metres), it was used as a rest room for the USAF authentication officer and the launch crew, and it was also used as an office for the missile systems analyst technician (MSAT). The squadron ORB for Bardney records that the annex there was affixed to the LCT during November and December 1960. It is also noted that hard work and carpentry by some squadron members continued despite the disconcerting news that the annex belonging to 142 Squadron at Coleby Grange had actually blown away.

Unless a countdown was in progress, power supplies to the LCA came from the site utility supply in the MEP building or, in the absence of this, the standby generator. Power supplied was at 480V AC 60-Hz routed to the PDT and then on to the launch emplacement skid-mounted power switchboard. The PDT also provided two feeds to the LCT, a 480V AC feed to supply the personnel heaters and a 120–208V AC supply for the lighting. Power for the LCT consoles was 28V DC, which was supplied from the launch emplacements by the EET.

Before a countdown was initiated, the trailer-mounted generators situated on the LCA were started up by means of a 'gen start' switch on the launch control officer's console, these then taking over the supply of power to the LCA and launch

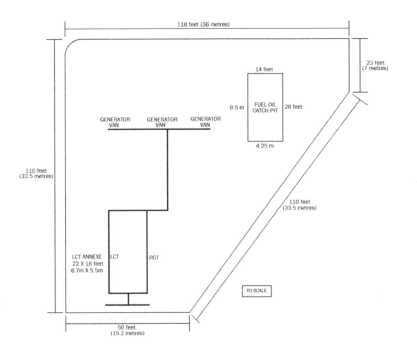

Above: The launch control area. Dimensions based on the Bardney site. (*Author's Collection*)

Below: LCA power supplies and distribution. (*Author's Collection*)

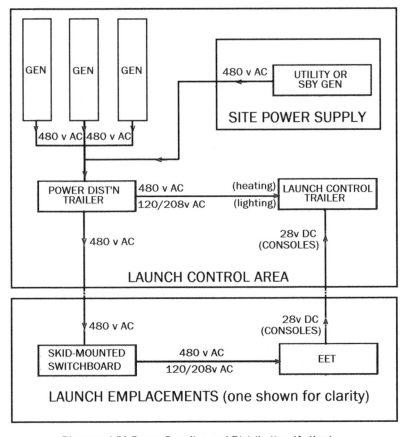

Diagram: LCA Power Supplies and Distribution. (Author)

emplacement. The generators, manufactured by General Electric, were driven by Cummins diesel engines. Each generator produced an output of 350 kilowatts at 480V AC 60 Hz. Rather than there being a generator for each emplacement, which would provide no redundant capability, the outputs of all three generators were synchronised, essentially producing a single feed possessing three sources.

The Launch Control Trailer

The countdown was controlled from the launch control trailer, which housed the consoles for the launch control officer and the three launch control console operators.

In addition to switches for generator start and the personnel heaters (which were switched off during the countdown), the LCO console comprised three identical launch panels, one for each missile. The panels are relatively self-explanatory, but of particular note is the phase timer clock, the missile status switch—which selected maintenance, checkout, and exercise or ready conditions (more of which later in the countdown)—and the two key slots, the launch sequence start switch, initiated by the turning of the LCO key, and the ominously marked war and peace switch, operated by the USAF AO during Phase 4 of the countdown. The annunciator lights indicated the current countdown phase and the missile status. It will be noted that the LCO could introduce an operational hold on the countdown sequence. The selection of an operational hold reset the phase timer, which would then time the period for which the countdown was held. The control and electronics assembly and hydraulics were switched off. In addition, the LOX tank vent valve was opened and all other propellant transfer system valves were 'failed safe'—that is, closed. Situated above the launch panels was a communications switchboard, and clearly, this needed to be handled with great care as the ORB for 106 Squadron at Bardney in January 1961 attests. Possibly with a hint of mischief, the squadron chronicler wrote:

> From an undisclosed source it would appear that a certain LCO engaged in dusting duties in the LCT entertained Bomber Command and Number 1 Group with a tuneful accompaniment to *Housewives' Choice* via the omnibus Telecoms circuit. It is not recorded if Bomber Command showed a suitable appreciation.

Housewives' Choice was a music programme, popular with ladies at home during the day. It was broadcast every morning from 1946 to 1967 on the BBC Light Programme. One can only begin to imagine the merciless banter to which the poor LCO concerned must have been subsequently subjected.

A launch control console operators console was provided for each missile. The console comprised two main elements: an upper console on which was situated the

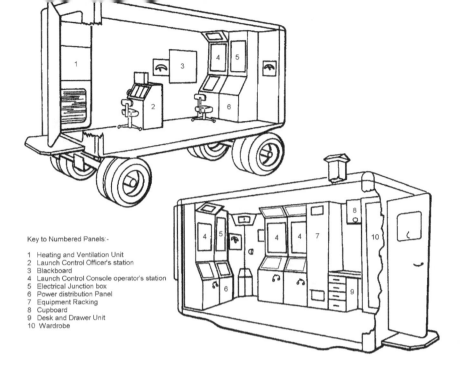

Launch Control Trailer.

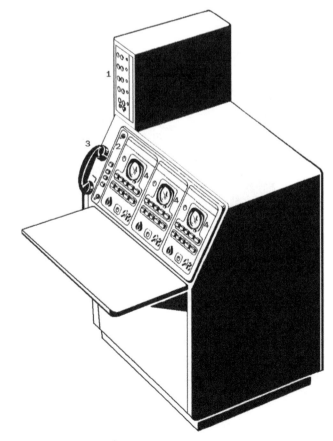

Right: Launch control officer's console, equipped with:
1. Communications switchboard.
2. Generator start panel.
3. Telephone handset.
4. Launch panel (three places).
   (*Author's Collection from USAF sources*)

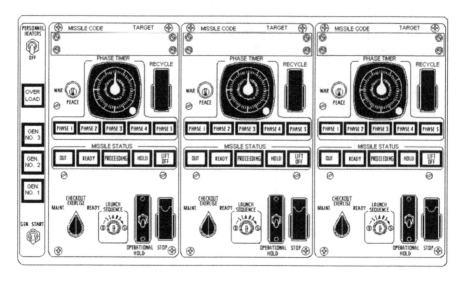

LAUNCH PANEL - LAUNCH CONTROL OFFICER'S CONSOLE

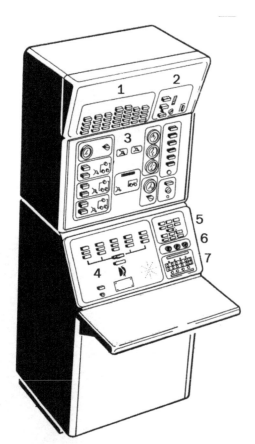

Left: Launch control console operator's console. Key to numbers:
1. Malfunction panel.
2. Target selection panel.
3. Guidance control.
4. Missile monitor panel.
5. Continuous use monitoring.
6. System override buttons.
7. Switchboard key unit. (*Author's Collection from USAF sources*)

malfunction panel, target selection panel, and the guidance control; and a lower console that housed the missile monitor panel, continuous status monitoring, override buttons, and a communications switchboard. The expanded countdown diagrams, it will be seen, have certain text boxes that are highlighted by means of a bold outline. The action in these boxes usually relates to the operation of a relay upon the satisfactory completion of a given set of conditions and the relays concerned are also shown in schematic form. A corresponding caption is generally to be found on the malfunction panel and this will remain illuminated should there be a malfunction in this series of events.

Other captions may be found elsewhere, for instance at the continuous status panel (LCCO console) or on the warhead monitor panel (EET). The target selector panel included a target selector switch, a switch to select the fusing of the warhead to the surface fuse or for an airburst, a timer abnormal annunciator, and a guarded target change switch. The target change switch could be used to cause a hold during phase three. The target change switch, if operated, would hold the countdown, but still allow the propellants to be loaded onto the missile to the 95 per cent LOX and 100 per cent fuel stage. After this, a technical hold could be introduced and the target change switch released.

The guidance control panel completed the upper console equipment. The functions of this panel have been covered as part of the guidance chapters and so are not described in any detail here. The left-hand column is for adjusting the potentiometer settings in the airborne guidance computer. The rotary switch at the top selects the meter to display the X, Y, or Z channel direction to zero. This indicated the direction to turn the potentiometer shafts, using the handset or slew switches, for the appropriate channel below the meter. The computer near zero lamp illuminated when the potentiometer was near the zero reference point and the computer on zero lamp illuminated when the zero reference point had been reached. The needle on the meter would be exactly central at this point. The X channel near zero gave the MECO signal, while the on zero would signal VECO. The next column contained switches for handing control to the EET, where the computer adjust operation as described above could be carried out at the velocity control. A timed sequence toggle switch is provided along with attitude vertical and airframe azimuth reference switches, which contained integral lights when operated. The yaw gimbal angle could be manually set from here—as could the reference for the guidance azimuth—to auxiliary or to theodolite. The alignment of the pitch, roll, and yaw gimbals could be seen, as could the nulling of the platform stabilisation gyros, once again by using a rotary switch to select the gyro for display. Finally, the guidance countdown can be monitored and guidance stop and reset switches are provided.

The missile monitor panel dominated the lower part of the console. This contained the display for the countdown and whether it was proceeding normally, was complete, or, exceptionally, proceeding abnormally, which it would do in certain circumstances. The technical hold switch could be operated to ensure that

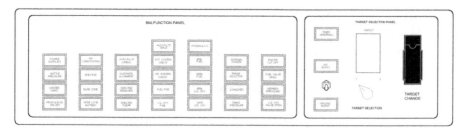

Malfunction and target selection panels. (*Author's Collection from USAF sources*)

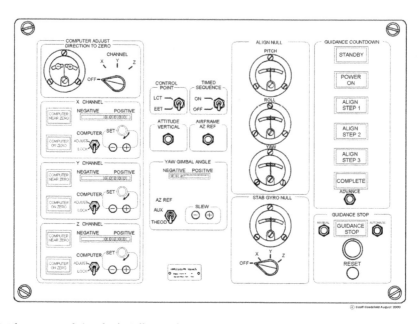

Guidance control. (*Author's Collection from USAF sources*)

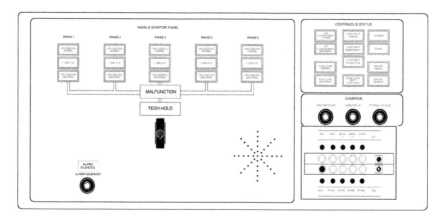

Missile monitor panel. (*Author's Collection from USAF sources*)

the countdown did not automatically resume upon a fault being rectified. The continuous status panel is self-explanatory, as is the communications switchboard.

The override buttons were operated to override parts of the sequence that had not signalled their completion and were to cover mainly mechanical operations that would deny the launch of an otherwise serviceable missile. In normal operation, the 'shelter removed' signal occurred at 93 feet into the retraction process and was one of the signals required to start the erector raising the missile to the vertical. At 192 feet, the shelter was fully retracted and the 'shelter clear' signal was forwarded to a relay ready for phase four. The shelter clear override button could be used to override a malfunction in the latter condition. The erector up override button could be used if the 'erector up and locked' signal was not received. If this relay did not operate, the phase two complete signal would not be sent. Provided that the missile was vertical, the erector up override could be pressed to complete the sequence. It was vital that the missile was indeed vertical otherwise fuel will start to flow into the missile in phase three, even with the missile at an angle. The propellant override button could be used to clear a fuel fine loading malfunction, provided the malfunction occurred after the completion of LOX fine loading. In a hold, the LOX would boil off, and this would eventually bring up a 95 per cent LOX malfunction signal, which could be countered by the use of the override button.

The Launch Countdown

The launch countdown was an automatic process consisting of five phases, during which the missile was checked, prepared, and finally launched. The LCO initiated the countdown by inserting and turning a key in the launch sequence key slot on the LCO console.

The countdown proceeded through each phase, during which a sequence of events must have been satisfactorily completed in order to proceed to the next phase. A time limit was applied to each phase to ensure that the required events had been completed within a reasonable time frame. If the timer timed out before the phase complete signal was received by the monitoring circuitry, an automatic hold would be imposed on the countdown at the point of the unsatisfactory event. The missile monitor panel on the LCCO console incorporated a safety feature in the form of a guarded switch, entitled technical hold, which, when operated, would prevent the countdown from resuming automatically upon the clearance of a fault. A much-simplified version of the major elements of the countdown appears below.

Standby
At standby, the missile lay horizontal within its shelter. Apart from the continuous heating of the guidance system gyros and the electronic monitoring of the nosecone, there was minimal equipment in use.

Phase One (Electronic)

Six minutes on phase timer, and four minutes to completion on average. This phase consisted mainly of checking circuitry and the switching on of systems.

Nosecone checked and prepare.

Flight control system switched on and hydraulics powered up, bringing the main sustainer and vernier engine thrust chambers up to centre.

Propellant transfer valves and sensors checked.

The RP-1 computer was powered.

Air conditioning switched on and air supplied to the missile engine and guidance sections.

Missile Nitrogen bottles pressurised.

Missile inertial guidance system aligned.

Engine circuitry prepared.

Phase Two (Mechanical)

Five minutes on Phase Timer, and three and a quarter minutes to completion on average.

Missile shelter retracted.

Flight control system checked by slewing main sustainer and vernier engines.

When the shelter reached 93 feet clear, the hydraulic pumping unit was started and the missile erected to the vertical.

Phase Three (Propellant Loading)

Six minutes on Phase Timer, and four minutes to completion on average.

Missile RP-1 fuel tank is loaded to 100 per cent capacity by RP-1 computer.

Missile LOX tank is loaded to 95 per cent capacity.

Clamshells open and transporter/erector is lowered.

Launch pins retract.

Phase Four (Electrical)

Exactly 115 seconds on Phase Timer, and seventy-five seconds to completion on average.

Missile inverter started and systems transfer to internal power.

Flight control system checked on internal power by the gimballing of the main sustainer and vernier engines.

Target selection checked.

Authentication officer's war and peace key turned to war.

Phase Five (Engine)

Exactly 115 seconds on Phase Timer, and ninety seconds to completion on average.

Missile LOX tank loaded to 100 per cent.

Missile RP-1 and LOX tanks pressurised.

Nosecone battery activated.

Start tanks pressurised.

Vernier engines started.

Gas generator and turbo pumps started.

Main sustainer engine ignition.

Missile lift-off.

The following pages expand on the sequence of events by means of a series of flow-charts. While these pages provide greater detail, it should be appreciated that it is still a simplified version, since, in many cases, the energising relays and signal paths are interdependent upon other relays and conditions that it was not possible to include in the diagrams.

Launch Countdown (Expanded)

The diagram shows the condition of a launch panel on the LCO console at the commencement of a countdown. The trailer-mounted generators have been started and are supplying power to the launch emplacements via the PDT. The LCO console is provided with 28V DC from the EET. The status selector switch was used to select the appropriate condition. The maintenance position, as its name implies, was used during routine maintenance and allowed countdown actions to proceed beyond the point where a live countdown would automatically stop due to non-occurrence of an event. It did this by simulating events and providing the signals indicating that the events had occurred. Having the switch in this position was the reason that a dual-propellant flow countdown (a countdown where the missile is filled with LOX and the RP-1 is diverted into a tanker) at 104 Squadron's base at Ludford Magna was able to continue all the way to the engine main LOX valve opening and discharge the LOX all over the pad, causing major damage. In check out and exercise, certain other conditions, such as shelter removal, the erector operation, and launch pin retraction, are simulated. The ready condition would be used for an actual launch and ensures that required actions do actually take place at the appropriate time in the sequence; otherwise the countdown will not proceed. This is the position the switch should have been in for the disastrous countdown at Ludford. Once the LCO's sequence start key was inserted and turned clockwise, relay K5301 received power and was energised. At the same time, a locking voltage, to keep the relay energised, was routed via a manual shutoff in the EET to the relay from the downstream side of the sequence key. The initiation of the countdown for the other two missiles was identical (diagram drawn by author).

The following expanded countdown pages commence with the phase one begin relay energised (all diagrams by the author).

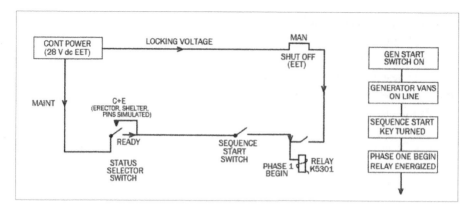

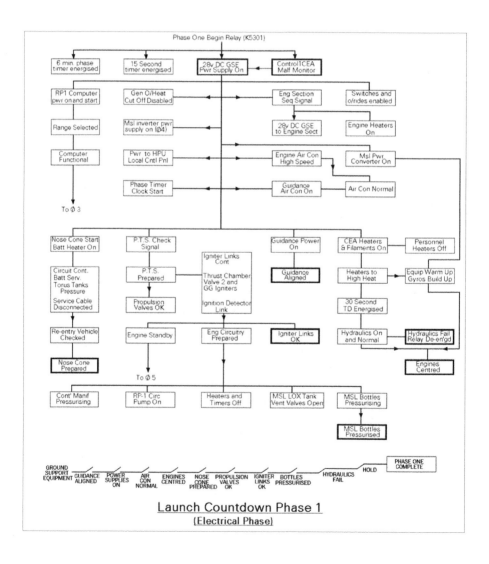

Launch Countdown Phase 1
(Electrical Phase)

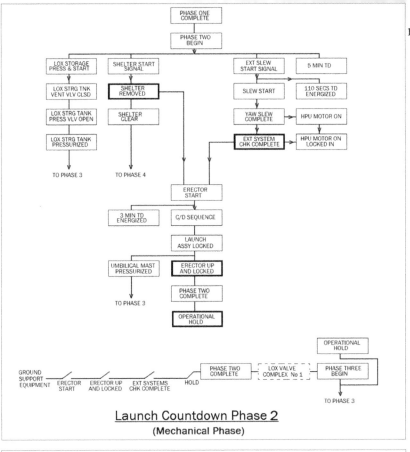

Launch Countdown Phase 2
(Mechanical Phase)

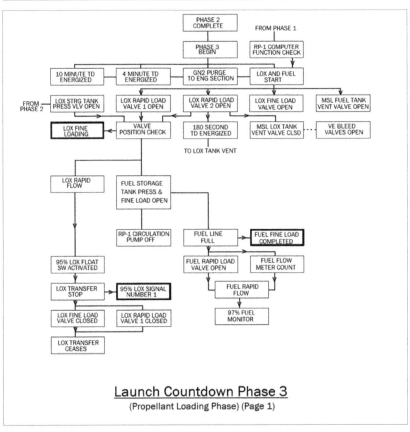

Launch Countdown Phase 3
(Propellant Loading Phase) (Page 1)

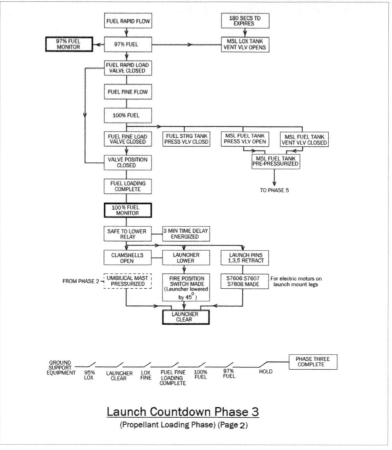

Launch Countdown Phase 3
(Propellant Loading Phase) (Page 2)

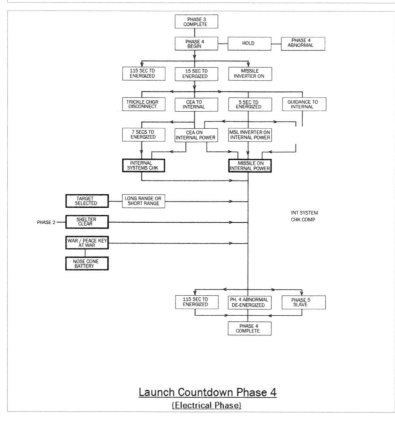

Launch Countdown Phase 4
(Electrical Phase)

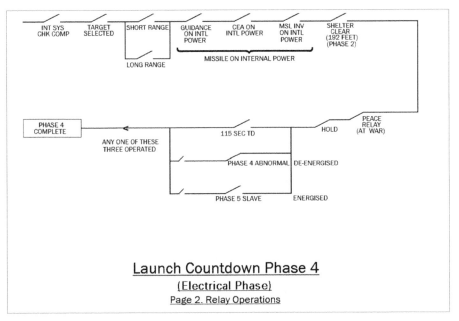

Launch Countdown Phase 4
(Electrical Phase)
Page 2. Relay Operations

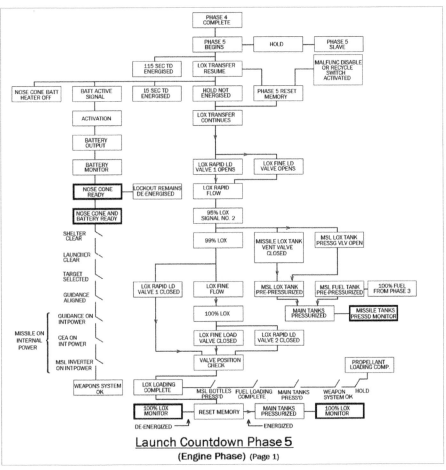

Launch Countdown Phase 5
(Engine Phase) (Page 1)

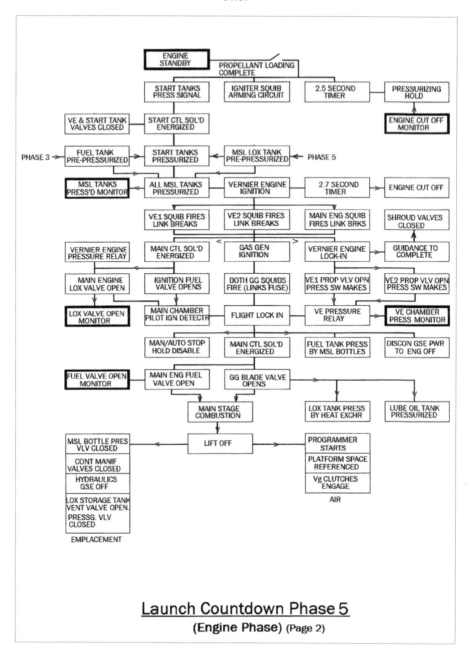

Launch Countdown Phase 5

(Engine Phase) (Page 2)

Epilogue

We have come to the end of our journey through Thor. The launch sites, a bustle of hyper-activity during their preparation—suddenly replaced by a cold and forbidding remoteness when declared operational—have now lain eerily silent for over fifty years. A number of Thor launch emplacements still remain; a few are largely intact, and at two sites (one still part of a military base) there has been afforded some small measure of legal protection. Long may they remain in place to remind us of their part in our Cold War heritage. It is sincerely hoped that the reader has enjoyed exploring the various aspects of the system and that this book has helped shed some light into the dark corners of those quiet remains, and, maybe, for a few moments at least, brought the sites, and Thor, back to life.

In the final edition of the Douglas Aircraft Company newsletter, *Airview News*, published monthly for DAC personnel deployed with Thor in the UK, Bill Duval, the Thor Deployment Manager, penned these last thoughts on the tremendous challenge that had been Project Emily. Although these words were written as Thor was being handed over to the RAF to begin her short career as a vital part of our nuclear deterrent, there is little doubt that they would still be faintly heard, echoing across twenty sites in the English countryside on the long summer evenings of 1963 as Thor's vigil drew to a close. It seems a fitting end to leave our story of Thor with the words of one of those who knew her best.

'A Final Word for Project Emily' by Bill Duval

Emily-A feminine personal name, according to Funk and Wagnell, but to those of us who have known Emily intimately, this is a pretty inadequate definition. Emily, to us, has been a gal of many moods, delightful at times and perfectly horrid on other occasions. She was a thing of beauty, an ugly wench, a lovely lady, a nagging shrew, a light-hearted child, a serious, worrying mother. She could be warm as a sunny summer's day, cold as a midwinter night, tender as the gentlest lover or harsh as the toughest gun-moll. Yet, in spite of her many faceted personality, I, for one, loved her … as I'm sure many of you did. She was, to say the least, an interesting female, and one we shall never forget. I am sad that the time has come to leave her.

Many thanks to all of you for your help in taking care of her during our whirlwind courtship.

Bibliography

Books

AP 3456, *Royal Air Force Manual* (London: Ministry of Defence, 2008, updated)
Boyes, J., *Project Emily: Thor IRBM and the RAF* (Stroud: Tempus Publishing, 2008)
Haart, J., *The Mighty Thor* (New York: Duell, Sloan and Pearce, 1961)
Mackenzie, D., *Inventing Accuracy* (London and Massachusetts: MIT Press, 1990)
TO21, Atlas ICBM, Missile Weapon System Technical Manual (USA: Periscope Film LLC, 2011)
TO21, Titan 1, Missile Weapon System Maintenance Manual (USA: Periscope Film LLC, 2011)
TO33, Technical Manual, Maintenance (USA: 1962)
Wynn, H., *RAF Nuclear Deterrent Forces* (London: The Stationery Office, 1994)

Archives

English Heritage (now Historic England)
The National Archives (TNA), Kew, London
US Patents Office

Periodicals and Miscellaneous

Airview News, Douglas Aircraft Company, (May 1960)
Aviation Week, December 1958.
Historic American Engineering Record of Space Launch Complex 10, US Army Research and Development Center, Construction (Engineering Research Laboratory, January 2002)
The Thor History, Douglas Missile and Space Systems, May 1963
Thor Test Booster for NASA Manned Space Capsule, Douglas Missile and Space Systems, NASA, May 1963
Flight
Flypast, April 2000
Lonquest, J. C., and Winkler, D. F., To Defend and Deter, USACERL Special Report, November 1996 (USA: Department of Defense, 1996)
Parker Temple III, Dr L., and Portanova, Dr P. L., 'Project Emily and Thor IRBM Readiness in the United Kingdom 1955-1960', *Air Power History*, Vol. 56, No. 3